OPPOSING VIEWPOINTS®
EXTREMIST GROUPS

Other Books of Related Interest

OPPOSING VIEWPOINTS®
EXTREMIST GROUPS

Karen F. Balkin, *Book Editor*

Bruce Glassman, *Vice President*
Bonnie Szumski, *Publisher*
Helen Cothran, *Managing Editor*

OPPOSING
VIEWPOINTS®
SERIES

GREENHAVEN PRESS
An imprint of Thomson Gale, a part of The Thomson Corporation

THOMSON
GALE

Detroit • New York • San Francisco • San Diego • New Haven, Conn.
Waterville, Maine • London • Munich

LIBRARY OF CONGRESS CATALOGING-IN-PUBLICATION DATA

Extremist groups / Karen F. Balkin, book editor.
   p. cm. — (Opposing viewpoints series)
Includes bibliographical references and index.
ISBN 0-7377-3594-5 (lib. : alk. paper) — ISBN 0-7377-3595-3 (pbk. : alk. paper)
   1. Radicals. 2. Radicalism. 3. Hate groups. I. Balkin, Karen, 1949– . II. Opposing viewpoints series (Unnumbered)
HN49.R33E9 2005
305.5'68—dc22   2004054127

Printed in the United States of America

"Congress shall make
no law...abridging the
freedom of speech, or of
the press."

First Amendment to the U.S. Constitution

The basic foundation of our democracy is the First
Amendment guarantee of freedom of expression.
The Opposing Viewpoints Series is dedicated to the
concept of this basic freedom and the idea that it is
more important to practice it than to enshrine it.

Contents

Why Consider Opposing Viewpoints?

"The only way in which a human being can make some approach to knowing the whole of a subject is by hearing what can be said about it by persons of every variety of opinion and studying all modes in which it can be looked at by every character of mind. No wise man ever acquired his wisdom in any mode but this."

John Stuart Mill

In our media-intensive culture it is not difficult to find differing opinions. Thousands of newspapers and magazines and dozens of radio and television talk shows resound with differing points of view. The difficulty lies in deciding which opinion to agree with and which "experts" seem the most credible. The more inundated we become with differing opinions and claims, the more essential it is to hone critical reading and thinking skills to evaluate these ideas. Opposing Viewpoints books address this problem directly by presenting stimulating debates that can be used to enhance and teach these skills. The varied opinions contained in each book examine many different aspects of a single issue. While examining these conveniently edited opposing views, readers can develop critical thinking skills such as the ability to compare and contrast authors' credibility, facts, argumentation styles, use of persuasive techniques, and other stylistic tools. In short, the Opposing Viewpoints Series is an ideal way to attain the higher-level thinking and reading skills so essential in a culture of diverse and contradictory opinions.

In addition to providing a tool for critical thinking, Opposing Viewpoints books challenge readers to question their own strongly held opinions and assumptions. Most people form their opinions on the basis of upbringing, peer pressure, and personal, cultural, or professional bias. By reading carefully balanced opposing views, readers must directly confront new ideas as well as the opinions of those with whom they disagree. This is not to simplistically argue that

9

everyone who reads opposing views will—or should—change his or her opinion. Instead, the series enhances readers' understanding of their own views by encouraging confrontation with opposing ideas. Careful examination of others' views can lead to the readers' understanding of the logical inconsistencies in their own opinions, perspective on why they hold an opinion, and the consideration of the possibility that their opinion requires further evaluation.

Evaluating Other Opinions

To ensure that this type of examination occurs, Opposing Viewpoints books present all types of opinions. Prominent spokespeople on different sides of each issue as well as well-known professionals from many disciplines challenge the reader. An additional goal of the series is to provide a forum for other, less known, or even unpopular viewpoints. The opinion of an ordinary person who has had to make the decision to cut off life support from a terminally ill relative, for example, may be just as valuable and provide just as much insight as a medical ethicist's professional opinion. The editors have two additional purposes in including these less known views. One, the editors encourage readers to respect others' opinions—even when not enhanced by professional credibility. It is only by reading or listening to and objectively evaluating others' ideas that one can determine whether they are worthy of consideration. Two, the inclusion of such viewpoints encourages the important critical thinking skill of objectively evaluating an author's credentials and bias. This evaluation will illuminate an author's reasons for taking a particular stance on an issue and will aid in readers' evaluation of the author's ideas.

It is our hope that these books will give readers a deeper understanding of the issues debated and an appreciation of the complexity of even seemingly simple issues when good and honest people disagree. This awareness is particularly important in a democratic society such as ours in which people enter into public debate to determine the common good. Those with whom one disagrees should not be regarded as enemies but rather as people whose views deserve careful examination and may shed light on one's own.

Thomas Jefferson once said that "difference of opinion leads to inquiry, and inquiry to truth." Jefferson, a broadly educated man, argued that "if a nation expects to be ignorant and free . . . it expects what never was and never will be." As individuals and as a nation, it is imperative that we consider the opinions of others and examine them with skill and discernment. The Opposing Viewpoints Series is intended to help readers achieve this goal.

David L. Bender and Bruno Leone,
Founders

Greenhaven Press anthologies primarily consist of previously published material taken from a variety of sources, including periodicals, books, scholarly journals, newspapers, government documents, and position papers from private and public organizations. These original sources are often edited for length and to ensure their accessibility for a young adult audience. The anthology editors also change the original titles of these works in order to clearly present the main thesis of each viewpoint and to explicitly indicate the opinion presented in the viewpoint. These alterations are made in consideration of both the reading and comprehension levels of a young adult audience. Every effort is made to ensure that Greenhaven Press accurately reflects the original intent of the authors included in this anthology.

Introduction

"The Internet is allowing the White supremacy movement to reach places it never reached before—middle and upper middle-class, college bound teens."
—Mark Potok, editor of Intelligence Watch for the Southern Poverty Law Center

Originally conceived as a useful tool for scientists and researchers, the Internet has become the wonder of the communications world. It is used for the legitimate purposes of exchanging information, research, and commerce. It has also been put to use as a vehicle for theft, sabotage, illegal gambling, and pornography. Extremist groups—especially white supremacists—have found the Internet to be a valuable resource in disseminating their messages of hate. Indeed, the Internet has changed the face of extremism in the United States and around the world.

In 1985 the Anti-Defamation League published "Computerized Networks of Hate," a report that described a computerized bulletin board that was created for and by white supremacists. Aryan Nations, a racist group affiliated with the pseudo-theological Identity Church hate movement, was responsible for the bulletin board. "White Pride Worldwide" was the slogan Stephen Donald Black used ten years later when, in 1995, he launched the world's first racist Web site—Stormfront. Black, a former member of the Ku Klux Klan, learned about computers while in federal prison in Texas. When he was released, he used his knowledge to create a Web site that encouraged racial separation. Referring to the Internet, Black says, "There is the potential here to reach millions. I don't know if it's the ultimate solution to developing a white rights movement in this country, but it's certainly a significant advance."

According to the Anti-Defamation League, the Aryan Nations' bulletin board served the white supremacist movement in the same ways that Stormfront did in its early days—and still does—and that more sophisticated Web sites do today: They were all designed to attract young people to the hate movement, stir up hatred against the enemies of the white race, help earn money for the movement through advertising and donations, provide a means to circulate secret, coded messages among extremists, and bypass the laws that nations have passed to stop hate literature from coming into their countries. Rabbi Abraham Cooper, associate dean of the Simon Wiesenthal Center, an organization that promotes religious tolerance, estimates that in 1999 there were over fourteen hundred Web sites spreading racist ideology and promoting racial or religious violence. Experts estimate that by 2001, the number had grown to as many as three thousand.

Children and teens are groups specifically targeted for influence by extremist Web sites. With their bold graphics and quick links, hate sites are created to appeal to young people. Some sites use racist rock music to pull in teens, others use word games and puzzles with white supremacist themes to catch the attention of younger Web-savvy children. "What the Net does for the [supremacist] movement is amplify its propaganda and recruiting reach," says Mark Potok, editor of *Intelligence Watch*, a publication of the extremist watchdog group Southern Poverty Law Center. "It's the perfect venue for recruiting middle-class and upper-middle-class young people. They're looking for kids to build a political movement and a revolution." In addition to influencing young people with racist propaganda, white supremacist Web sites promote violence. While it is often difficult to show a direct link between regular viewing of hate sites and actual violence perpetrated against racial or religious minorities, most racist sites encourage violence and applaud violent acts. When John Williams King, a white racist, was convicted of beating and dragging to death James Byrd, a black man, one white supremacist Web site called King an "American hero" and asked readers to "give thanks to God" for Byrd's murder. Aryan Nations' Web site originator Black claims that he does not want to incite violence with his Web site, but notes that it would be "disingenuous" of him to reject violence between the races "because history is based on wars."

Despite the proliferation of hate sites, many analysts warn against efforts to shut them down. Anthony Pratkanis, a social psychology professor at the University of California at

Santa Cruz, who has done extensive studies on propaganda and hate groups, argues that it is difficult to hold a Web site responsible for inspiring violence unless there is a provable conspiracy against a specific group. Potok comments, "You can't sue someone or prosecute them for creating an atmosphere of hate. Those things are simply protected by the First Amendment." He argues further that hate sites serve as a safety valve, allowing the majority of racists to vent their frustrations on the Web instead of in violent acts. "I don't think suppressing free speech helps," Potok says. "It actually plugs up the safety valve to some extent." Moreover, Internet service providers, not bound by the First Amendment to accept all content, can refuse any Web site they find objectionable. Filters and parental scrutiny are the best answers for parents seeking to protect their children from hate sites.

Authors in *Opposing Viewpoints: Extremist Groups* debate issues that surround the social problems created when extremist groups clash with the rest of society in the following chapters: Are Some Religious Groups Harmful? Do Some Liberal Groups Benefit Society? Do White Supremacist Groups Promote Hate and Violence? What Extremist Groups Pose a Threat Worldwide? While the views of all groups are protected in the United States, extremist groups often push the limits of the law, earning them the scrutiny of law enforcement, politicians, the media, and countless social commentators.

Chapter Preface

Christian Identity is a religious movement that unites many white supremacist groups throughout the United States. The movement has its roots in the British-Israelism beliefs of the nineteenth century, which held that the white race, specifically the Anglo-Saxon, Celtic, Scandinavian, and Germanic peoples, are the racial descendents of the tribes of Israel and God's true chosen people. Christian Identity espouses a variant of Christian fundamentalism mixed with virulent racism and anti-Semitism that encourages violence. In the last decade Identity followers have been tied to murder, robbery, and kidnapping, and the group is on the FBI's list of most dangerous hate groups. Identity followers are frequently members of militia groups, who stockpile food and weapons preparing for a racial Armageddon.

David Nelwert, author of *In God's Country: The Patriot Movement and the Pacific Northwest*, argues that Christian Identity is the link that connects many otherwise distinct and geographically separate extremist groups. Nelwert maintains, "Adherence to [Christian Identity] is probably the single greatest common denominator among all the various fragmented factions of the radical right wing in America. It is practiced by the neo-Nazis of the Aryan Nations, by the leaders of the Militia of Montana, and by the remnants of the Ku Klux Klan in the South." Leonard Zeskind, president of the Institute for Research and Education on Human Rights and a leading analyst of white supremacist movements, agrees with Nelwert, saying that he sees "a merger of Christian nationalism with white nationalism" occurring in the United States.

Though actual numbers of Christian Identity followers are difficult to obtain, Rosemary Radford Ruether, professor of applied theology at the Garrett Evangelical Theological Seminary at Northwestern University, estimates that there are about fifty thousand hardcore adherents who would call themselves Identity Christians. However, she claims that the numbers of adherents could be growing due to the Internet. She writes, "[Identity Christians] have recently targeted alienated white youth in affluent suburbs and have considerable presence through a number of Web sites and the promotion of racist music aimed at youth." According to the Southern Poverty Law Center, an organization that monitors extremist groups, racist Web sites and extremist rock music—often with racist or anti-Semitic lyrics—are two of the most common methods hate groups use to expand their membership by reaching young people.

Christian Identity is a racist, anti-Semitic theology that is practiced by many white supremacist groups. In the following chapter authors debate the effect of religious extremist groups on the social fabric of the United States.

"*Many who call themselves Christian . . .
teach a racist theology that is not only . . .
unacceptable to mainstream Christianity,
but also poses tangible dangers to society.*"

Religion Is Easily Exploited by Extremist Groups

Matthew C. Ogilvie

Racist Christian groups pose a spiritual danger to all Christians and a physical threat to everyone who does not agree with them, Matthew C. Ogilvie argues in the following viewpoint. According to Ogilvie, racist Christians use religion to justify and further their causes. Religion, he maintains, can goad people to action, for good or ill. Matthew C. Ogilvie is an assistant professor of systematic theology at the University of Dallas in Irving, Texas.

As you read, consider the following questions:
1. The combination of which two factors in racist Christianity is cause for concern, in the author's opinion?
2. According to Ogilvie, why do racist Christians preach a theology of rebellion against gun control?
3. What arguments does Ogilvie maintain are put forth by the World Church of the Creator to justify using religion as a vehicle for race ideology?

Matthew C. Ogilvie, "Children of a White God: A Study of Racist 'Christian' Theologies," *Human Nature Daily Review*, http://human-nature.com/nibbs/01/ogilvie.html, vol. 1, October 23, 2001. Reproduced by permission of the publisher and the author.

It is common knowledge that Islamic extremism has been associated with numerous terrorist attacks around the world. It remains, though, that racist Christian theologies have also animated violent movements. One key example concerns the Oklahoma City bombing. Bomber Timothy McVeigh has been connected to white supremacist movements such as White Aryan Resistance and the Christian Identity movement, both of which promote racist theology. In Australia, racist theologies have gained attention through the medium of racist politician Pauline Hanson. Apart from her generally anti-Indigenous and anti-Asian stance, Hanson has advocated giving preference to Christian migrants over those from non-Christian backgrounds. The media attention given Ms Hanson has been accompanied by an increase in race-based violence within Australia. While one acknowledges that Ms Hanson has not articulated a "race-theology" her movement has brought out many others who do present such racist religion.

The seriousness of the threat presented by supremacist groups is reflected in the US Army's approach to anti-terrorism. In the prepublication edition of *Force Protection: Antiterrorism 1997*, it is noted that there exists within the United States, "an eclectic array of extremist organizations, which do not officially condone terrorism but may serve as breeding grounds for terrorist activities." Of those extremist groups, there are those that either espouse supremacist causes, or foster discrimination or the deprivation of civil rights based on race or religion. What concerns us most is the combination of the powerful factors of supremacist feeling and race discrimination with a militaristic attitude. With that combination, race-based theologies have turned from parlour talk into matters of life and death. Of much concern is that white racists, who call themselves "Christian" and who believe in a theology that gives divine justification to their beliefs, possess arsenals of high-technology weapons, the likes of which many Middle-East terrorists would be most jealous.

Racist Christians and the Pro-Gun Lobby

Racist theology has today found itself powerful and influential voices. Of these, most prominent would be David Duke, former Ku Klux Klan leader, who was elected to the Louisiana House of Representatives. Duke proclaims that he has always been a believing Christian and that an integral part of his Christianity has been a theology of racial segregation. We read in his own work that in the name of race preservation, God has commanded genocide, segregation and anti-miscegenation, and today forbids racial intermarriage and the crossing of racial boundaries. Duke's views are certainly on the fringe of Christian thinking, but he is only the visible voice of a wider movement of people whose theology conceives violence, hate, intimidation and race conflict to be in the name of God.

In studying racist theologies, one is also struck by the connection between the racist Christians and extreme elements of the pro-gun lobby. In his reflections on "Race and Christianity," Duke proceeds directly from proposing racial segregation to outlining a theology of gun possession, in which he proclaims Christ's command for his followers to possess guns. The Christian Identity movement also follows such teaching, simultaneously demanding of its followers a theology of racial separation and a belief in Christ's command for Christians to own and be ready to use the most advanced available weapons of their day, such as an M-16 assault rifle. In addition to these beliefs, we note that racist Christians generally preach a theology of rebellion against gun control, on the grounds that it is part of a "New World Order," which is supposed to be an anti-White, anti-American and anti-Christian movement. While we shall discuss these beliefs in detail below, it should suffice for our introduction to note that there are many who call themselves Christian and who teach a racist theology that is not only intellectually unacceptable to mainstream Christianity, but also poses tangible dangers to society. . . .

Biblical Fundamentalism

Racist Christianity shares with Biblical fundamentalism a naive realist approach to scripture. This parallel should not surprise us, because many, if not most or all, racist Christians align themselves to fundamentalist Churches. While we would in no way wish to implicate most fundamentalists in racism, the fact remains that the fundamentalist method is both attractive to and has had great impact on the way that racists use their sources. Besides using an exegesis by naive realism, we would note several other characteristics common to both groups.

First, racist Christians and fundamentalists hold common views on evolution. On evolution, [Baptist minister] Bob Jones presents the fundamentalist position by declaring that, "The process of the human race has not been upward from the swamp by evolution, but downward from the garden by sin." Also from a strictly creationist viewpoint, [creationist writer and lecturer John] Mackay declares that "The current cultural status of the races . . . is a direct consequence of whether the ancestors of any race worshipped the living God, or deliberately rejected Him. There is no such thing as a primitive race evolving upwards." With fundamentalists, racist Christians believe that creation can only go backwards, not forwards. Properly speaking, the fundamentalist theory of human development is of actual devolution, rather than possible evolution. Likewise, racists believe that God has made white people as they are, and that one cannot develop positively either whites or any other race. One must either maintain one's race in stasis, or face the downward spiral of ungodly devolution.

Fear of Change

The first point ties in with our second, namely, that fundamentalism and racist Christianity are extremely negative towards human creativity. Fundamentalists exercise an extreme form of Calvinism, holding that nothing that proceeds from the nature of man can be of any goodness. Taking up Calvin's idea that all proceeding from unregenerate human nature is damnable, fundamentalists hold that only that which comes from regenerated humanity, which in practice means from within the fundamentalist fold, can be of benefit to humankind. Likewise, racist Christianity holds that nothing humankind can do to or for itself can bring about effective improvement to ourselves. We have seen in this article how racists fear race-mixing and intermarriage. The underlying assumption behind such fear is that any change to humanity will inevitably be for the worse.

This racist fear of any change contradicts Christian theology that sees human stewardship of God's creation as meaning that we are co-creators with God. This belief is reflected, in part, by the Genesis creation account's statement that God has commanded humanity to fill the earth, and subdue it, which suggests making some improvements to the earth. An oft-ignored part of Christian theology also concerns the issue of procreation. Unfortunately, the furore over contraception in Catholicism has seen the theology of procreation more often ignored or misunderstood. Understood fully, procreation refers not only to biological conception, but to the whole process and life self-giving of generating, nurturing and educating a child. Procreation thus concerns the responsibility and right of parents to bring forth and take on the ongoing care of their child. Such stewardship effectively makes parents co-creators with God. We propose that Christians would have little trouble in extending this positive theology from parent-child relationships to a theology of the entire human race's co-creation with God of itself. One can thus engender a more positive outlook on divine-human relationships than those envisaged by racism or fundamentalism.

Counter-Modern Suspicion

Thirdly, both fundamentalism and racist Christianity share a counter-modern suspicion. Racists are likely to regard modern society as intolerant and dogmatic, due to its opposition to racist ideology. As modern history, biology, theology, philosophy all provide sharp and resolute criticisms of racist thinking, it is no surprise that racists should oppose all things modern. Fundamentalists are also practically defined by their opposition to modernity, especially the modern embrace of liberal culture and religion. We may be familiar with the fundamentalist hatred for liberalism, which often translates into contempt or hatred for liberals. However, there is here significant deviation of racist Christianity from fundamentalism. Regarding fundamentalism, we find upon serious reading, that despite its abhorrence of liberalism, fundamentalism most often is defined by liberalism. By this point, we mean that from the very start, Biblical fundamentalism has been defined by its opposition to matters such as evolutionary science, critical scholarship of the Bible, and liberal, pluralist morality. [Ed] Dobson and [Ed] Hindson lend support to this idea in their discussion of the history of American fundamentalism. They introduce their work [*The Fundamentalist Phenomenon*] by noting that they shall evaluate the impact of fundamentalism by reference, among other things, to its "War with Liberalism." They also admit that, to understand fundamentalism and place it in its correct perspective, they have to deal with liberalism. The term "War with Liberalism" is Dobson and Hindson's and is the title of a chapter in their book. That "war," in practical terms, defines fundamentalism. Apart from brief references to "the Fundamentals" fundamentalists are more inclined to deal with their efforts to combat what they saw as increasing corruption and anti-Christianity in an increasingly liberal Church. Dobson and Hindson effectively define the genesis of fundamentalism by its rise as a "unified, organized effort to combat its [liberalism's] influence."

Ramirez. © 1999 by Copley News Service. Reproduced by permission.

Racist Christianity, on the other hand, though as thoroughly anti-modern as fundamentalism, is opposed to modern, liberal culture for different reasons. In the first place, racism did not start as a specific reaction to increasing liberalism. Moreover, racist Christianity does not appear to have functionally defined itself so much by its opposition to new developments in society. This is not to say that racist Christianity is not a reactive, anti-modern movement in the same way as fundamentalism. Rather, racist Christianity has its own agenda, its own identity and its own objectives. The degree and manner in which it reacts to society is defined in fairly narrow terms, as opposed to fundamentalism, which has become counter-cultural in very broad terms.

Religion as a Racist Tool

The critical observer will readily agree with our observation that racist Christianity does not derive its doctrines from an impartial reading of its sources. Race theology is, more properly speaking, not a theology so much as a predetermined ideology expressed in words commonly used within Christian theology. To be truthful, racist Christianity, though using the power of religion and religious language, does not originate within a religious context, but a social and political context that uses religion for its own purposes.

We may ask why racists use religion to further their aims. The anti-Christian World Church of the Creator (WCOTC) [which now calls itself the Creativity Movement] provides candid reasons why religion is chosen as the vehicle for race ideology. In the first place, while a political party may have some influence over part of a person's life, religion dominates all parts of a person's life. The genuinely religious person will have sublated by his or her religion all of one's life decisions concerning morality, work and economy, law, education, marriage, family and community life. Another aspect of religion is that, when firmly established, it can outlast even the most dogged of political parties or social groups. While political parties last rarely longer than a century, the well-established religion can have influence for centuries after the death of its founder.

A Cover for Moral Evils

Further insight into why religion can [be] used as a racist tool comes from the master of social manipulation. In *Mein Kampf*,

[Adolf] Hitler gave his assessment of religion's significance by stating: "Verily a man cannot serve two masters. And I consider the foundation or destruction of a religion far greater than the foundation or destruction of a state, let alone a party." Hitler went on to observe that religion can be an effective cover, even for the otherwise obvious vices of those who hide beneath religion's mantle. That religion can be used as a cover for moral evils raises for us the whole question of religious freedom. We would note that the great majority of racist Christianities have originated in the United States, a nation in which freedom of religion is sacrosanct. Unfortunately, the strength of this constitutional right, along with a certain vagueness as to what exactly constitutes a "religion" has meant that, in practical terms, "freedom of religion" has meant the right to preach any form of corruption or madness, regardless of its rationality, social implications or other concerns. Various movements repeatedly find protection from criticism, public scrutiny or proactive legal action because they fall under the mantle of "free" religions. If Hitler is right in his observations on the baser side of human nature, and his wicked success gives us every reason to think so, then we have to address seriously the question of what manner of freedom we allow religions. If we are to subject racist religions to open scrutiny, and call these faiths to account, then we must abandon the popular notion of freedom of religion as a relativist right to pursue any belief system whatsoever. Rather, one would propose a more serious notion of religious freedom as freedom from state or other coercion. That is, rather than the licence to create any form of anti-social movement, one proposes that religious freedom be conceived as the right to uncoerced worship, which right brings with it the responsibility to be reasonable and rational, and responsible towards people and society.

If we turn back to why religion is so useful to racist religionists, Hitler again provides us with helpful, even if unpalatable, reflections. Religion proves potent at controlling people's actions, Hitler surmises, because "The great masses of people do not consist of philosophers; precisely for the masses, faith is often the sole foundation of a moral attitude." Later Hitler repeated the point by claiming that the

"Churches and church leaders must take this [white supremacist] movement seriously, particularly given its religion-based ideologies that promote hatred and violence."

Religion Can Counter Violent Extremism

David Ostendorf

Churches are countering racist Christian theology within their communities and throughout the United States, David Ostendorf, a United Church of Christ minister and the director of the Center for New Community in Oak Park, Illinois, argues in the following viewpoint. Because many racists use religion to justify their beliefs, church leaders are in a unique position to turn the tables using the positive power of religion against the hate and violence these white supremacist groups promote. He insists that leaders mobilize their congregations and their communities to fight the bigotry that masquerades as religion.

As you read, consider the following questions:
1. According to Ostendorf, what Christian heresy grew out of nineteenth-century British Israelism?
2. Why is it a serious mistake to ignore white supremacist activity, in the author's opinion?
3. What are some of the rules that Ostendorf suggests communities should follow when they respond to hate groups?

David Ostendorf, "Countering Hatred," *The Christian Century*, vol. 116, September 8, 1999, p. 861. Copyright © 1999 by the Christian Century Foundation. Reproduced by permission.

In a nine-state area of the Midwest, 272 far-right-wing organizations—including Christian Identity, Christian Patriot, neo-Nazi and Ku Klux Klan groups—ply their racist and anti-Semitic ideologies. Hundreds of other groups are known to operate nationally, involving tens of thousands of true believers and their followers. Violence can and does erupt from their ranks, as was evident in August [1999] when former Aryan Nations security officer Buford Furrow went on a shooting rampage at a Jewish day-care center in Los Angeles and then murdered a Filipino-American postal worker.

Roots of Hatred

Religion-based hatred is the engine of the violent far-right; dreams of a white Christian homeland, free of the despised "Zionist Occupation Government," is its volatile fuel. Most of these groups have roots in the racist and anti-Semitic ideology of Christian Identity, a Christian heresy that grew out of 19th-century British Israelism. (An exception to this pattern is the World Church of the Creator [Creativity Movement], organizational home of Benjamin Smith, who in July [1999] went on a shooting spree in Illinois and Indiana, targeting minorities.)

British Israelism was advanced in the U.S. by Henry Ford and given its peculiar American twist by Wesley Swift, who founded the Church of Jesus Christ Christian in 1946. William Potter Gale, a Swift convert, shaped the racist tenets of the ideology and helped birth the Posse Commitatus, the violent arm of the movement. . . .

Organized Opposition Is Needed

But a new generation of Identity leaders has emerged . . . and is advancing the racist and anti-Semitic ideology far beyond the Aryan Nation compound. In congregations scattered across the country, and in homes and other gathering places, Identity believers worship as the "true Israel," the chosen white race. A core group of Identity pastors, including Pete Peters of LaPorte, Colorado, has spread the message of the movement. In 1992 Peters gathered some of the nation's leading white supremacists and neo-Nazis at Estes Park, Colorado, for a meeting that launched the militia movement.

Because the white supremacist movement is organized in

countless communities, its opponents need to be organized. One example of an effective response to white supremacist activity is the work of clergy in Quincy, Illinois. Quincy is a Mississippi River town of 41,000 that serves as a center of commerce for the region. This past February [1999], when clergy learned that Pete Peters was planning a March "Scriptures for America" seminar in Quincy, the ministers met to plan their response.

Immediately after the meeting, a small delegation of clergy went to the motel where the seminar was scheduled to be held. The ministers told the motel managers about the nature of the event. The managers were shocked and immediately canceled it. While the motel suffered a financial loss, its owners and managers were adamant about not providing a place for racism and anti-Semitism to be brazenly taught.

The Quincy Ministerial Association did not stop there. It organized a Sunday afternoon education event, "From Hate to Community," and held it at the same motel Peters had intended to use. Participants in this seminar were encouraged to have dinner at the motel dining room as a show of support and appreciation for the managers' actions. Seventy-five religious and community leaders participated in the seminar, which was widely advertised in church bulletins and by local media.

Standing up to white-sheeted Klansmen is one thing. It can be much more difficult to counter white-shirted Identity or neo-Nazi leaders. These may be, after all, the folk with whom we work and worship, folk who are not blatantly racist and anti-Semitic, whose stance on government or guns may seem within the realm of mainstream politics. They may not even know that their movement is rooted in the ideology of Christian Identity.

Hate Groups Must Not Be Ignored

It is, in any case, a serious mistake to ignore white supremacist activity, hoping that it will simply go away. The argument that "they will just get more press if we openly oppose them" does not hold up and has costly consequences.

Media will report on white supremacist activity, regardless of how the community responds. Media will also report—and hunger for—the story of how a community organizes its responses. When communities do not respond, the likelihood of repeated or increased white supremacist activity escalates. Failing to build public, moral barriers against hate is an open invitation to hate groups. The key to diluting its expansion and appeal is naming names, and fully exposing this racist and anti-Semitic movement to the light of day.

Kansas church leaders have practiced this kind of intervention for years, and have recently pooled their experience and commitment in a coalition with civic organizations in

---

The Positive Effect of Religion

Americans strongly correlate religion with individual morality and behavior, considering it one of very few antidotes to the moral decline they observe in our nation today. That's particularly important since people are increasingly alarmed by what many consider a national moral crisis caused by such factors as a declining family structure, disappearing politeness and civility and rising materialism.

Americans believe that if individuals were more religious, their behavior would improve and our society would be stronger as a result. Crime, teen pregnancy, divorce, greed, uncaring parents, unfeeling neighbors—Americans believe that such problems would be mitigated if people were more religious. And to most citizens, it doesn't matter which religion it is. In fact, for over half (53%) of those surveyed, being religious means "making sure that one's behavior and day-to-day actions match one's faith," not attending religious services or even feeling the presence of God.

In short, people equate religion with personal ethics and morality. And as a result, seven in ten (70%) Americans want religion's influence on American society to grow. However, alongside this strong conviction that religion benefits society is an equally strong adherence to a respect for religious diversity that translates into a surprising tolerance of other people's beliefs and practices. This is no mere lip service on the public's part, nor is it an abstract ideal that disintegrates the moment it is tested. Americans seem to have an ingrained expectation that they will encounter people with different ideas about religion in their daily lives, and the idea of tolerance is so well accepted that it has been absorbed into daily standards for social conduct.

Deborah Wadsworth, "For Goodness' Sake: Why So Many Want Religion to Play a Greater Role in American Life," Public Agenda Survey, 2001.

Kansas City and Topeka. The Kansas Area Conference of the United Methodist Church has been particularly outspoken in countering Christian Identity and the militia movement in rural areas of the state. Kansas Ecumenical Ministries is an important partner in this effort. In cooperation with the Mainstream Coalition, Concerned Citizens of Topeka and the Jewish Community Relations Bureau, a longstanding ally in the struggle against organized hate group activity in Kansas, religious and civic leaders are exploring new strategies to curtail this movement.

Churches and church leaders must take this movement seriously, particularly given its religion-based ideologies that promote hatred and violence. The need is all the more urgent as movement leaders become adept at recruiting youth through music and other entry points. White supremacist bands travel the country, and their compact discs can be found in suburban record stores. Their links to the National Socialist movement are now complete with William Pierce's acquisition of Resistance Records, the nation's largest distributor of white supremacist music. Pierce, a neo-Nazi, is the author of *The Turner Diaries*, the book that inspired the Oklahoma City bombing.

When responding to hate groups, communities should remember these rules: Document the problem, expose the group, and stay informed about its local activities. Create a moral barrier against hate by speaking out and by organizing counter-responses. Build coalitions and seek to keep those coalitions together for the long haul to counter racism, anti-Semitism, bigotry and scapegoating. Assist the victims. Reach out to the constituencies targeted for recruitment. Target the entire community, including youth, for education and action. Remember that hate groups are not a fringe phenomenon. Seek to address broad social, economic and racial concerns.

Religious Leaders Must Stand Against Hate

Several years ago a friend participated in a peaceful protest that directly confronted a white supremacist group. Until that point the city leaders had decided to stay as far away from the group as possible. They held a unity rally and then hoped that the haters would be ignored.

Following the protest my friend, an experienced labor organizer, called me up and in an unusually subdued voice reported that she had never in her life felt the presence of evil as she did that day. She had looked around for moral support and counsel from the religious community, but found no one. No religious leaders were present to stand with her and others against the evil.

Anastasis. Resurrection. To stand against the forces of death. That's what we are called to do in the face of this hateful and violent racist movement, which often offers a twisted version of the Christian faith.

> *"On campuses across this country . . . are organizations that promote the culture of Islamic terrorism and its . . . anti-American agendas."*

Islamic Fundamentalists in the United States Pose a Serious Threat

David Horowitz

David Horowitz argues in the following viewpoint that radical Islamic fundamentalist groups organize on university campuses, promote anti-American agendas, and lure idealistic students into terrorist activities. He maintains that one such group, the Muslim Student Association (MSA), routinely invites pro-terrorist, anti-democratic speakers to campuses where it operates. Further, under the guise of social activism, the MSA encourages impressionable American students to become involved in Islamic-sponsored, anti-Western terrorism, usually directed against Israel. David Horowitz is a nationally known writer and political activist.

As you read, consider the following questions:

1. According to the author, why did the Black Panthers disintegrate in the 1970s?
2. What group does Horowitz argue has become the Black Panthers of the contemporary antiwar movement?
3. What is the purpose of the International Solidarity Campaign, in Horowitz's opinion?

When I was a college radical and anti-war activist forty years ago, I was quite the intellectual and (in my estimation) cautious and sober. Though I became an editor and then co-editor of the leading radical magazine of the Sixties, *Ramparts*, I never threw a rock during the entire era. I never joined a radical sect and never went to Communist Cuba or North Vietnam, which were then the meccas of the radical faith. Although I was a founder of an organization called the "Vietnam Solidarity Campaign," I never fooled myself that the Communist state that would result from an American defeat would be a "rice roots democracy," the way Tom Hayden and other leaders of the "New Left" movement proclaimed.

Nonetheless, before the era was over, I was lured by my desire to do humanitarian good and to further the cause of social justice into working with the Black Panthers, a group of radical gangsters who in 1974 murdered a friend of mine (the mother of three children) and a dozen other individuals besides. The project I had become involved in with the Panthers was building an elementary school.

From the vantage of the political and cultural left, my activities with the Black Panthers were neither marginal [n]or extreme. At the time, the Panthers were icons of the progressive intellectuals, symbolizing strong black leaders who were standing up for their "oppressed" community. The entire liberal culture supported them. Leading cultural figures like Garry Wills and Murray Kempton were writing praises of the Panthers in the *New York Times* Sunday magazine. Kempton even compared their leader Huey Newton to Mahatma Gandhi and Martin Luther in the *Times'* august pages. To this day *The New York Times*, *The Washington Post* and other pillars of the American political culture, celebrate the Panthers—the murderers of my friend and a dozen others—as icons of the "social struggle."

Radical Groups Promote Islamic Terrorism

Fortunately, the Panthers disintegrated in the early Seventies, dragged down by their criminal activities, internecine battles and the sordid brutality of their leaders, Huey Newton and Eldridge Cleaver. Before he died, Cleaver told a *Sixty*

Minutes audience, "If people had listened to Huey Newton and me in the Sixties, there would have been a holocaust in this country." Many radicals, among them Cleaver's most prominent promoter—*Los Angles Times* columnist Robert Scheer—looked forward to that holocaust and actively encouraged it. The Panthers were the "noble savages" of liberal compassion, symbols of the injustice that America was said to be inflicting on American blacks.

What would have happened if the Panthers had remained intact to the present? What if they had been the arm of an international terror network whose goal was the destruction of the United States? There are such groups in America today. They are radical groups who identify with the violent *jihad* [holy war] of Islamacist terror organizations like al-Qaeda, Hizbollah, Islamic Jihad and Hamas. And they have the support of a radical culture that regards America as the Great Satan, and Muslims and Arabs as the people whom America oppresses.

On campuses across this country, embedded in the leadership of every radical "anti-war" protest group, are organizations that promote the culture of Islamic terrorism and its anti-Western, anti-Israeli and anti-American agendas. One that will serve as an example for the others is the radical Muslim Student Association (MSA). The Muslim Student Association is an organization financed by the Saudis and also by student funds at every university where it operates. The ideas and enthusiasms that it promotes among impressionable college students should give every American cause for concern.

On October 22, 2000, Ahmed Shama, president of the UCLA [University of California, Los Angeles] Muslim Students Association led a crowd of demonstrators at the Israeli consulate in chants of "Death to Israel!" and "Death to the Jews!" Shama declared that [Israeli leader] Ehud Barak, [Palestinian leader] Yassir Arafat and [U.S. president] Bill Clinton were all "racist zionists." "When we see that a peace process is being negotiated between Zionists, mediated by Zionists, controlled by Zionists, and being portrayed in the media by Zionists, we come and we condemn all of you," Shama said.

Militant Islam Is a Threat to the United States

The Muslim population in this country is not like any other group, for it includes within it a substantial body of people—many times more numerous than the agents of [terrorist] Osama bin Ladin—who share with the suicide hijackers a hatred of the United States and the desire, ultimately, to transform it into a nation living under the strictures of militant Islam. Although not responsible for the atrocities [on September 11, 2001], they harbor designs for this country that warrant urgent and serious attention.

In June 1991, Siraj Wahaj, a black convert to Islam and the recipient of some of the American community's highest honors, had the privilege of becoming the first Muslim to deliver the daily prayer in the U.S. House of Representatives. On that occasion he recited from the Qur'an and appealed to the Almighty to guide American leaders "and grant them righteousness and wisdom."

A little over a year later, addressing an audience of New Jersey Muslims, the same Wahaj articulated a rather different vision from his mild and moderate invocation in the House. If only Muslims were more clever politically, he told his New Jersey listeners, they could take over the United States and replace its constitutional government with a caliphate. "If we were united and strong, we'd elect our own emir [leader] and give allegiance to him. . . . [T]ake my word, if 6–8 million Muslims unite in America, the country will come to us." In 1995, Wahaj served as a character witness for Omar Abdel Rahman in the trial that found that blind sheikh guilty of conspiracy to overthrow the government of the United States. More alarming still, the U.S. attorney for New York listed Wahaj as one of the "unindicted persons who may be alleged as co-conspirators" in the sheikh's case.

Daniel Pipes, *Commentary*, November 2001.

Pro-Terrorist Speakers

One of the invited speakers at the event was Hamid Ayloush, a member of the Council on American-Islamic Relations (CAIR), which was also an event sponsor. In his speech, Ayloush solicited contributions for the Holy Land Foundation, an organization that the Justice Department has shut down as [a] funder of al-Qaeda.

On May 26, 2001 the UCLA Muslim Student Association held a conference of Islamic radicals on the UCLA campus.

The conference featured speakers from CAIR whose founder is a supporter of the terrorist organization Hamas, and the Muslim Public Affairs council, a radical group whose executive director has justified the terrorist killing of 243 U.S. marines in Lebanon in 1983 by Hizbollah suicide bombers: "This attack, for all the pain it caused, was not in a strict sense, a terrorist operation. It was a military operation, producing no civilian casualties—exactly the kind of attack that Americans might have lauded had it been directed against Washington's enemies."

The UCLA Muslim Student Association has routinely invited pro-terrorist speakers to the UCLA campus and paid for them with student funds. At a January 21, 2001 event, nine months before 9/11, a speaker called Imam Musa, an African-American Muslim who is a staple of the anti-war rallies staged in Washington DC declared: "If you were to say that the Soviet Union was wiped off the face of the earth . . . people would have thought you were crazy, right? The people of Afghanistan didn't have the intellect or historical knowledge to know that they wasn't supposed to wipe out the Soviet Union, is that right? . . . We saw the fall of one so-called superpower, Old Sam is next."[1]

Praising Bin Laden

Prior to [the September 11, 2001, terrorist attacks] the UCLA magazine *Al-Talib* featured a cover story on [al-Qaeda leader] Osama Bin Laden titled, "The Spirit of Jihad." The editorial declares:

> When we hear someone refer to the great mujahideen Osama Bin-Ladin as a 'terrorist' we should defend our brother and refer to him as a freedom fighter; someone who has forsaken wealth and power to fight in Allah's cause and speak out against oppressors. We take these stances only to please Allah.

Two days before 9/11, *Al-Talib* co-sponsored a dinner at [the] University of California, Irvine to honor then accused (and subsequently convicted) cop-killer (and Imam [religious leader]) Jamil Al-Amin—aka H. Rap Brown. Another cop-

1. The Soviet Union occupied Afghanistan from 1979 to 1989.

killer favored by Muslim student groups and by the anti-war movement generally is Mumia Abu Jamal. Imam Musa spoke here as well:

> You think Zionism and Palestine is the only dictatorial power in the world. We're telling you about apartheid right here in America. . . . When you fight Old Sam, you are fighting someone that is superior in criminality and Nazism. The American criminalizer is the most skillful oppressor that the world has ever known.

The Palestinian terrorists have become the Black Panthers of the contemporary anti-war movement. The leftwing culture celebrates the suicide bombers of women and children as desperate victims of Jewish oppression. Attackers and destroyers of the Oslo peace process [between the Palestinians and Israelis] are proclaimed as heroes. Terrorists and totalitarian radicals are lionized as fighters for social justice. Israelis and Americans are condemned as Nazis.

Students Are Seduced by Terrorism

How many American college students and anti-war activists have been seduced by these poisonous elements at work in our society? It is difficult to know. But one who has already paid for it with her life is Rachel Corrie, a 24 year old undergraduate at Evergreen College in Olympia Washington, who has become known as the "Saint of Rafiah," the name of the West Bank town where she died. Evergreen is one of the many leftwing campuses in America, whose values have been turned so upside down by tenured leftists that it recently featured convicted murderer Mumia Abu Jamal as its commencement speaker. (He spoke via tape [because he is in prison]).

Rachel Corrie began her activist career as a member of the Olympia Movement for Justice and Peace, an organization formed directly after the 9/11 attack on America to oppose an American military response. Its members feared that, "America would retaliate by bombing some of the poorest and most oppressed on earth, the Afghan people."[2] Their Marxist view of the world is captured in one of the

2. According to the George W. Bush administration, Afghanistan harbored al-Qaeda, the terrorist group responsible for the September 11 attacks.

Movement's favored slogans: "Corporate Globalization Equals Imperialist Domination."

It was not long after she joined the Olympia Movement that Rachel Corrie was burning an American flag in the name of social justice. It was logical step for her to gravitate to an organization that would demonstrate her commitment to the cause. Through her contacts in the anti-war movement she joined the International Solidarity Campaign, whose purpose is to recruit young Americans to become human shields for Palestinian terrorists. The Solidarity Campaign's ties to terrorism became inescapable eleven days after Rachel Corrie's death when an elite anti-terror unit of the Israeli Defense Forces captured a senior Islamic Jihad terrorist, Shadi Sukiya hiding in its offices in Jenin.

Rachel Corrie was sent by International Solidarity to a town called Rafiah in the Gaza Strip to obstruct Israeli Defense Forces conducting anti-terror operations. She sat down in front of an Israeli military bulldozer, and—according to an American eyewitness—was inadvertently killed when the machine, whose driver could not see her, ran over her. . . . The *New York Times Magazine*—the same magazine that once celebrated the murderer of my friend by the Black Panthers—had a tribute to Rachel Corrie, to her humanitarian goodwill. The article was called "One Last Sit-In," to wrap the halo of Martin Luther King and the civil rights movement around her pro-terrorist activities. The *Times* article summarized the news reports of Corrie's death in these words: "23-year-old peace activist from Olympia, Wash., crushed to death by an Israeli Army bulldozer as she tried to block the demolition of a physician's home in Gaza."

"Major Arab and Muslim organizations issued statements strongly condemning the [terrorist] attacks [by Arabs against the United States]."

Most Followers of Islam in the United States Reject Terrorism

Shibley Telhami

Shibley Telhami argues in the following viewpoint that, like all Americans, Arab and Muslim Americans are horrified by the September 11, 2001, terrorist attacks on the United States and are seeking solutions to terrorism. Further, Telhami insists that a majority of Arab Americans—69 percent—are in favor of "an all-out war against countries which harbor or aid terrorists." Moreover, while many Arab Americans report racial profiling since the attacks, 54 percent believe that extra questioning of people with Middle Eastern accents or facial features by police is justified. Shibley Telhami is the Anwar Sadat Professor at the University of Maryland.

As you read, consider the following questions:
1. According to Telhami, from which countries do most Arab Americans come?
2. Who was the first sitting president to speak at conferences of Arab-American organizations, according to the author?
3. In Telhami's opinion, on what issue are Arab Americans in almost complete agreement?

Shibley Telhami, "Arab and Muslim America: A Snapshot," *The Brookings Review*, vol. 20, Winter 2002, pp. 14–15. Copyright © 2002 by The Brookings Institution. Reproduced by permission.

In a *New York Times* article appearing a week after the horror [of the terrorist attacks] that befell America on September 11, [2001,] a Muslim woman described her dilemma this way: "I am so used to thinking about myself as a New Yorker that it took me a few days to begin to see myself as a stranger might: a Muslim woman, an outsider, perhaps an enemy of the city. Before last week, I had thought of myself as a lawyer, a feminist, a wife, a sister, a friend, a woman on the street. Now I begin to see myself as a brown woman who bears a vague resemblance to the images of terrorists we see on television and in the newspapers. I can only imagine how much more difficult it is for men who look like [terrorists] Mohamed Atta or Osama bin Laden."

Excruciating moments like those the nation experienced [in] September [2001] test the identity of all Americans, but especially those whose identity may be caught in the middle. Many Arab and Muslim Americans lost loved ones and friends in the attacks in New York and Washington, and others had loved ones dispatched to Afghanistan as American soldiers to punish those who perpetrated the horror (Muslims are the largest minority religion in the U.S. armed forces). But many also had double fears for their own children. On the one hand, they shared the fears of all Americans about the new risks of terror; on the other, they were gripped by the haunting fear of their children being humiliated in school for who they are.

Two Partially Overlapping Communities

There is much that's misunderstood about Arabs and Muslims in America. Although the two communities share a great deal, they differ significantly in their make-up. Most Arabs in America are not Muslim, and most Muslims are not Arabs. Most Arab Americans came from Lebanon and Syria, in several waves of immigration beginning at the outset of the 20th century. Most Muslim Americans are African American or from South Asia. Many of the early Arab immigrants assimilated well in American society. Arab-American organizations are fond of highlighting prominent Americans of at least partial Arab descent. Ralph Nader, George Mitchell, John Sununu, Donna Shalala, Spencer Abraham, Bobby Rahal, Doug

Flutie, Jacques Nasser, Paul Anka, Frank Zappa, Paula Abdul, among many others. Like other ethnic groups in America, Arabs and Muslims have produced many successful Americans whose ethnic background is merely an afterthought.

Arab Americans now number more than 3 million, Muslims roughly 6 million (though estimates range from 3 million to 10 million). The income of Arab Americans is among the highest of any American ethnic group—second only to that of Jewish Americans. Arab Americans have become increasingly politicized over the years. According to a recent survey, proportionately more Arab Americans contribute to presidential candidates than any other ethnic group—and the groups surveyed included Asian Americans, Italian Americans, African Americans, Hispanic Americans, and Jewish Americans. Over the past decade especially, Arab-American political clout has increased. Although Arab Americans were long shunned by political candidates, President [Bill] Clinton became the first sitting president to speak at conferences of Arab-American organizations, and both President Clinton and President [George W.] Bush have normalized ongoing consultations with Arab- and Muslim-American leaders. In the fall 2000 election, presidential candidates sought the support of Arab Americans, not only for campaign contributions, but also as swing voters in key states, especially Michigan. The September 11 tragedy, coming just as Arab-American political clout was ascendant, has provided a real test for the community's role in American society and politics.

The Impact of September 11

For Arab and Muslim leaders, the terrorist crisis has been like no other. It has forced them to contemplate profoundly their identity. Are they Arabs and Muslims living in America, or are they Americans with Arab and Muslim background? The answer came within hours after the terrorist attacks. Major Arab and Muslim organizations issued statements strongly condemning the attacks, refusing to allow their typical frustrations with issues of American policy in the Middle East to become linked to their rejection of the terror. Rarely have Arab and Muslim organizations in the United States been so assertive.

The enormity of the horror, the Middle Eastern background of the terrorists, and the terrorists' attempt to use religion to justify their acts have inevitably led to episodes of discrimination against Arabs and Muslims, as well as against those, such as Sikhs, who resemble them. But the support that both Arabs and Muslims received from thousands of people and organizations far outweighed the negative reaction. Arab and Muslim organizations were flooded with letters and calls of empathy from leaders and ordinary Americans, including many Jewish Americans, for most understood that at stake were the civil liberties of all Americans.

Muslim American Leader Condemns Terrorism

The president of the American Muslim Council, Yahia Basha, has praised President [George W.] Bush for his swift, decisive steps to declare war on terrorism and simultaneously protect the Muslim American and Arab American communities from ethnic backlash following the September 11 [2001] terrorist attacks. . . .

"When the United States got attacked, we Muslim Americans felt we ourselves had been violated. We lost many people in those attacks. We are American. We are here as part of this nation," Basha said. . . .

Basha said members of the Muslim and Arab communities in the United States have stepped forward with offers to help U.S. law enforcement agencies combat the terrorist threat.

"Muslim Americans and Arab Americans have volunteered their knowledge of languages and other things to American law enforcement agencies to help them catch terrorists and fight terrorism. We support in any way we can the campaign against terrorism. I don't think any human being or religion could justify those crimes," Basha said.

He said the true teachings of Islam have nothing to do with violence and terrorism.

U.S. Department of State International Information Programs, "Muslim American Leader Condemns Terrorism," October 9, 2001.

In large part, the public reaction was a product of quick decisions and statements by President Bush and members of his cabinet, members of Congress from both parties, and local political leaders. The president in particular acted quickly to make two central points that seem to have resonated with most of the public. The first was that the terrorists did not represent Islam and that Osama bin Laden must not be allowed to turn his terror into a conflict between Islam and the West. The second was that Muslim and Arab Americans are loyal Americans whose rights must be respected. Bush's early appearance at a Washington, D.C., mosque with Muslim-American leaders underlined the message.

The President Acted Correctly

The message seems to have gotten through. Despite the fears that many Americans now associate with people of Middle-Eastern background, a survey conducted in late October [2001] by Zogby International found that most Americans view the Muslim religion positively and that the vast majority of Arabs and Muslims approve the president's handling of the crisis. (Among Arab Americans, 83 percent give President Bush a positive performance rating.) Moreover, 69 percent of Arab Americans support "an all-out war against countries which harbor or aid terrorists."

Certainly, the events of September 11 will intensify the debate within the Arab and Muslim communities in America about who they are and what their priorities should be. One thing is already clear. Although both communities have asserted their American identity as never before and although 65 percent of Arab Americans feel embarrassed because the attacks were apparently committed by people from Arab countries, their pride in their heritage has not diminished. The October survey found that 88 percent of Arab Americans are extremely proud of their heritage. So far, however, the terrorist attacks have not affected the priorities of the Arab public in America as might be expected, given Arab Americans' deep fear of discrimination.

Support for Profiling

Typically, Arab-American organizations highlight such domestic issues as secret evidence and racial profiling and such foreign policy issues as Jerusalem, Iraq, and the Palestinian-Israeli conflict. While Arab Americans, like other minorities, are involved in all American issues and are divided as Democrats and Republicans, as groups they inevitably focus on issues about which they tend to agree. The situation is no different from that of American Jews, who are also diverse, but whose organizations largely focus on issues of common interest.

Given the fear of profiling that Arab Americans had even before September, one would expect this issue to have become central for most of them since September 11. And for many it certainly has. Arab-American organizations, especially, have focused on it. But the findings of the Zogby poll among Arab Americans in October were surprising. Although 32 percent of Arab Americans reported having personally experienced discrimination in the past because of their ethnicity, and although 37 percent said they or their family members had experienced discrimination since September 11, 36 percent nevertheless supported profiling of Arab Americans, while 58 percent did not. Surprisingly, 54 percent of Arab Americans believed that law enforcement officials are justified in engaging in extra questioning and inspections of people with Middle Eastern accents or features.

Palestinian-Israeli Dispute Must Be Resolved

Though their views on profiling have been mixed since September 11, Arab Americans have been considerably more unanimous on one subject—the need to resolve the Palestinian-Israeli dispute. Seventy-eight percent of those surveyed agreed that "a U.S. commitment to settle the Israeli-Palestinian dispute would help the president's efforts in the war against terrorism." Although most Arab Americans are Christian and mostly from Lebanon and Syria—and only a minority are Palestinians—their collective consciousness has been affected by the Palestinian issue in the same way that Arab consciousness in the Middle East has been affected. In a survey I commissioned in five Arab states (Lebanon, Syria, United Arab Emirates, Saudi Arabia, and Egypt) . . . majorities in each country consistently ranked the Palestinian issue as "the single most important issue to them personally." The role of this issue in the collective consciousness of many Arabs and Muslims worldwide is akin to the role that Israel has come to play in contemporary Jewish identity.

Like all Americans since September 11, Arab and Muslim Americans are searching for solutions to terrorism. Like all Americans, they are also finding new meaning in aspects of their identity to which they might have given little thought a few short months ago.

> *"Christian nationalists seek to eviscerate the
> capacity of federal courts to protect the
> religious freedom and equality of all
> Americans."*

The Religious Right Has a Harmful Agenda

Frederick Clarkson

The religious Right seeks to restore a Christian constitution that never existed, promoting their political vision of the United States as a Christian nation, Frederick Clarkson maintains in the following viewpoint. Clarkson argues that the religious Right's notion of the United States as a Christian theocracy has no historical basis and is in direct opposition to the Constitution. He contends that the religious Right is trying to undermine religious freedom in America. Frederick Clarkson is the author of *Eternal Hostility: The Struggle Between Theocracy and Democracy*. He also writes for the *Christian Science Monitor.*

As you read, consider the following questions:

1. Why is Roy Moore called "the Ten Commandments judge," in Clarkson's opinion?
2. According to the author, what would the Constitutional Restoration Act do?
3. What action does Clarkson argue was a judicial break with Christian America?

Was the United States founded as a "Christian nation"? For many conservative Christians there is no question about it. In fact, this is one of the primary ideas animating and informing the Christian right in the US. We are likely to hear a great deal about it this election year [2004]—thanks to Roy Moore, the former chief justice of the Alabama Supreme Court, who is at the center of a national campaign to alter the course of history. Depending on whom you talk to, Mr. Moore is alternately a hero, a crackpot, or a demagogue.

Whatever one's view, Moore, known to many as "the Ten Commandments judge," has come to personify a revisionist view of American history—one that, if it gains wide currency, threatens to erode the culture, and constitutional principle, of religious pluralism in the US.

Moore's story is already the stuff of legend. After being elected chief justice, he had a 5,280-pound monument to the Ten Commandments installed in the rotunda of Alabama's state judicial building in 2001. Moore insisted he had a First Amendment right to "acknowledge God" as the "moral foundation of law." The result of the inevitable lawsuit was US District Judge Myron Thompson's decision that Moore had violated the establishment clause of the First Amendment by creating "a religious sanctuary within the walls of a courthouse." When Moore refused to remove the rock, he was removed from office.

Judge Thompson got it right. But Moore and his allies see the decision as a defining moment in their campaign to "overthrow judicial tyranny." At stake over the long haul is the authority of the courts to protect individual civil rights against religious and political majoritarianism.

Constitution Restoration Act

On one front, leaders on the Christian Right are organizing Ten Commandments rallies across the country. The charismatic Moore is often the headliner. A recent rally in Dallas drew 5,000 people. Meanwhile in Congress, US Rep. Robert Aderholt and Sen. Richard Shelby, both of Alabama, have introduced a bill (written by Moore and his lawyer) that would remove jurisdiction from the federal courts over all matters involving the "acknowledgement of God" in the public arena, including school prayer, the pledge of allegiance, and the posting of the Ten Commandments in public buildings. The Constitution Restoration Act would be retroactive, apparently to undo many federal and Supreme Court decisions—such as Moore's case.

While the bill is unlikely to pass this year, it does suggest the emerging contours of the debate.[1]

Although Moore's movement has gained some political traction, its core premise has a fundamental flaw: It aims to "restore" a Christian constitution that never existed. And this presents challenges for Moore and his allies as they attempt to invoke the framers of the Constitution in support of their contemporary notions of a Biblically based society.

Last August, for example, James Dobson, head of Focus on the Family, rallied with Moore in front of the Alabama state courthouse.

"I checked yesterday with my research team," Dr. Dobson announced. "There are only two references to religion in the Constitution." The first, from the preamble, he said, refers to securing "the blessings of liberty," which, he asserted, "came from God" (although there is nothing in the document to support that view.) The other was the First Amendment's establishment clause that, he said, "has given such occasion for mischief by the Supreme Court."

Disestablishment of Christian Churches

However, Dobson's researchers missed—or ignored—Article Six of the Constitution. That's the one barring religious tests for public office and set in motion disestablishment of the Christian churches that had served as arbiters of colonial citizenship and government for 150 years.

Mainstream historian Gary Wills writes that the framers' major innovation was "disestablishment."

"No other government in the history of the world," he writes, "had launched itself without the help of officially recognized gods and their state connected ministers."

Christian Right historian Gary North agrees. The ratifica-

---

1. The bill did not pass.

The Religious Right's Scorecard for Congress

The graphs and tables below tell a story. They portray a Congress that is highly polarized, and they dispel two important myths:

Myth 1) There isn't much difference between the two political parties.

Myth 2) The Religious Right has grown into obscurity.

According to ratings of key organizations of the Religious Right, members of Congress who support their agenda overwhelmingly dominate the Republican Party. The following graph is based on how Christian Coalition rated the United States Senate in 2001, the most recent year their scorecards for the U.S. Senate are available.

U.S. Senate—2001
Christian Coalition Scorecard

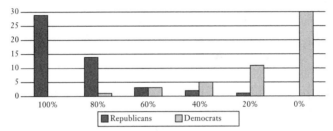

29 Senators voted with Christian Coalition 100% of the time. They were all Republican. 30 Senators received a 0 rating from Christian Coalition meaning they never voted with their issues. They were all Democrat.

U.S. House of Representatives—2001
Christian Coalition Scorecard

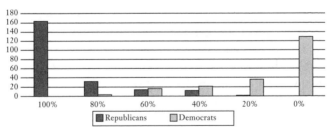

163 Republicans and 1 Democrat received scores of 100%. 32 Republicans and 3 Democrats received scores of 80%. 16 Republicans and 14 Democrats received scores of 60%. 12 Republicans and 22 Democrats received 40%. 1 Republican and 36 Democrats received 20%. 129 Democrats and no Republicans received 0.

"Scorecards: Snapshots of Congress," www.4religious-right.info, May 1, 2004.

tion of the Constitution was a "judicial break with Christian America." Article Six provided a "legal barrier to Christian theocracy" leading "directly to the rise of religious pluralism," he declares in *Political Polytheism: The Myth of Pluralism*. Indeed, history shows that the framers of the Constitution sought to establish religious equality among citizens and in government. But, as Christian nationalists seek to eviscerate the capacity of federal courts to protect the religious freedom and equality of all Americans, we can expect that one of their main tactics and goals will continue to be the revision of history itself.

"The religious Right has acted as an often lonely source of resistance to the complete triumph of relativism in our culture and libertinism in our behavior."

The Religious Right Has a Beneficial Agenda

Norman Podhoretz

In the following viewpoint Norman Podhoretz insists that there is no reason to fear that the religious Right is trying to make the United States into a Christian theocracy or has any other harmful agenda. On the contrary, Podhertz argues that the religious Right offers many positive virtues. He maintains that conservative Christian communities help maintain standards of behavior and offer staunch resistance to the triumph of relativism in American culture. Norman Podhoretz is a nationally known author and former editor of *Commentary* magazine.

As you read, consider the following questions:
1. In Podhoretz's opinion, why are Jewish people more likely to fear the Christian Right than other groups?
2. According to the author, why did fundamentalist Christians become politically involved?
3. What is the basis for Podhoretz's argument that liberals are not as unhappy with the Christian Right as they profess to be?

Norman Podhoretz, "Essay: The Christian Right and Its Demonizers," *National Review*, April 3, 2000. Copyright © 2000 by National Review, Inc., 215 Lexington Avenue, New York, NY 10016. Reproduced by permission.

Who's afraid of the religious Right? Not I. And yet, as a "New York intellectual," I am precisely the type of person who is supposed to be trembling with apprehension at the baneful influence conservative Christians have gained within the Republican party and, through it, on the nation as a whole.

Of course, though to the manner born, I am not a typical New York intellectual. Most members of my breed are situated somewhere left of center, and I have long since migrated to a position on the other side of the political divide. Yet even the tiny handful of my former fellows who so much as barely tolerate my apostasy, at least in certain of its aspects, still taunt me with a classic piece of black humor: "Other than that, Mrs. Lincoln, how did you like the play?"

The "that" in the case of this "Mrs. Lincoln" refers to the alleged extremism and bigotry for which John McCain recently attacked [fundamentalists] Pat Robertson and Jerry Falwell. That speech may have destroyed McCain's chances of beating George W. Bush in the presidential primaries. And yet he was only saying out loud what is believed by vast numbers of the non-Republican-independents and crossover Democrats—on whom he had been counting to carry him to the nomination [for president in 2000].

Why then did the speech do him damage? The answer is that any gains he may have made with these voters could not compensate for the losses he sustained among others who, whether religious or not, are not strict secularists. In fact, even many Catholics seem to have resented McCain's assault on Robertson and Falwell, since they took it as an attack on the role of religion in general in our politics. On this point, the old sectarian animosities were trumped by a growing tendency among Catholics and Protestants to view seriousness about "traditional values" as more important than the specific theological etiology of that seriousness.

Fear of the Christian Right

But not, I would be willing to bet, among Jews. Now, like many New York intellectuals (though not quite so many as is often imagined), I am Jewish. This makes my attitude doubly untypical. Indeed, a good guess would be that an even higher percentage of American Jews in general than of New York intellectuals (Jewish or not) are afraid of the Christian Right.

As Jews, my coreligionists are responding in part to inherited—and well-grounded—ancestral anxieties over the prevalence of anti-Semitism in conservative Christian circles. Never mind that, in the justly celebrated quip of Irving Kristol (a New York Jewish intellectual who preceded me in the political migration from left to right), Christians in America today are less interested in persecuting Jews than in marrying their sons and daughters. This undoubtedly poses a threat to what has come to be known as "Jewish continuity." But it is surely a benign one compared with the experience of the past, when Christian hostility toward Jews more often took forms ranging from discrimination to forced conversion, expulsion, and murder.

Never mind, too, that the charges of anti-Semitism which have been made against Pat Robertson are unsustainable. True, he has written a few off-the-wall things about an alleged conspiracy between Freemasons and Jewish bankers to take over the world in the 18th century. It is also true that he has sharply criticized "Jewish intellectuals and media activists" of today for playing a part in "the assault on Christianity."

Yet unlike the crackpot theory about the 18th century, his charge against the intellectuals and media activists of Jewish origin cannot so easily be dismissed. (It is important to recognize, however, that these particular persons tend to be the ones who have been described as "non-Jewish Jews.")

Furthermore, with regard to the concerns of present-day "Jewish Jews," Robertson has been a staunch friend. He has supported Israel through thick and thin; and when the Soviet Union still existed, he contributed large sums of money to help Jews emigrate. Would that all Christians were so anti-Semitic. . . .

Anti-Semitism Has Declined Among Christians

Speaking first as a Jew, even if I shared to some degree in the paranoid interpretation of the Christian Right's agenda, I would still not be afraid of it. For quite apart from the sharp decline of anti-Semitism among Christians, there seems to me not the remotest chance that any Supreme Court—not even one composed of five Antonin Scalias and four Clarence Thomases—would read the First Amendment's prohibition of "an establishment of religion" as sanctioning this country to be declared officially Christian.

Moreover, the paranoid interpretation in this instance has no more basis in reality than paranoia does in any other situation. Evangelical and fundamentalist Christians were once content to render unto Caesar what was Caesar's and to concentrate on saving their own souls. What drew them into politics, first behind Jerry Falwell's Moral Majority and then Pat Robertson's Christian Coalition, was not any wish to impose their own views and mores on the rest of us. On the contrary: Far from being an aggressive move, it was a defensive one. They were trying to protect their own communities from the aggressions the liberal culture was committing against them, with the aid of the courts, the federal bureaucracies, and the ubiquitous media.

The Religious Right Works for Human Good

The broader evangelical tradition, from which the Christian Right emerged, proved politically self-conscious and socially reformist from its beginnings in the early nineteenth century. Though evangelicals were as ideologically diverse then as they are now, there can be little doubt that many joined (if not led) the fight against slavery and the abuse of alcohol. Although the specific issues that the Christian Right has focused upon in the 1990s have changed—abortion, homosexuality, gun control, prayer in the schools—the important point to note is that a determination to reach out and construct or reconstruct society in terms of a larger image of human good has remained constant. One does not need to agree with all or even any of the Christian Right's prescriptions in order to see how profoundly American its missionary-like activism really is.

Grant Wacker, National Humanities Center, October 2000.

In this the Christian Right failed—so dismally that some of the people who persuaded them that political activism was the only way to defend themselves are now counseling an abandonment of that particular field and a retreat into the old insularity.

But now let me put on my intellectual's hat and explain why in that capacity I do not fear the Christian Right either. Take, to begin with, the cultural backwardness—in shorthand, the William Jennings Bryan anti-intellectual streak—that repels so many of my fellow intellectuals. Where an issue like the teaching of creationism is concerned, one does not need to be an uncritical Darwinist to think the intellectuals have a point—and the recent poll showing overwhelming support for including creationism in the curriculum makes that point stronger. But what the intellectuals ignore is that there has been a reversal of roles between the Bryan and [Clarence] Darrow traditions.[1] Nowadays a far greater threat to scientific progress and cultural freedom comes from the secular Left than from the religious Right—as witness the promulgation of speech codes on the campus, and the attempts there to proscribe any deviation from the officially approved line on subjects as diverse as IQ, homosexuality, and affirmative action.

Virtues of the Religious Right

But it would be dishonest of me to suggest that my attitude toward the religious Right is merely characterized by an absence of fear. For I must confess that I think this movement has certain positive virtues.

For one thing, the conservative Christian communities have served as a reminder of the religious foundations on which this country was established and on whose capital its democratic system still draws. And for another, the religious Right has acted as an often lonely source of resistance to the complete triumph of relativism in our culture and libertinism in our behavior.

On this latter issue, I have long suspected that there is a parallel between the attitudes of many liberals today and the way the French took shelter under the American nuclear umbrella during the Cold War while simultaneously gratifying themselves with luxuriant outbursts of contempt against us. Such liberals, I think, are not quite so unhappy as they

1. William Jennings Bryan and Clarence Darrow were opposing attorneys in the Scopes trial over the teaching of evolution in schools.

profess to be that there is a force in this country whose very existence helps set limits to libertine tendencies that they themselves worry about, especially when they have children, but that they do not know how to restrain and would lack the courage to fight even if they were in command of the necessary arguments. And so they rely on the "nuclear umbrella" of the Christian Right, while denouncing it all the more loudly as they quietly benefit from its protection.

"The JDL [attempts to] . . . change the Jewish image through sacrifice and through all necessary means . . . even strength, force and violence."

The Jewish Defense League Is Justified

Jewish Defense League

Jewish people have a right to defend themselves, their rights, property, institutions, and honor by any means necessary, including the most violent, the Jewish Defense League (JDL) argues in the following viewpoint. The organization maintains that its use of violence is justified by the attacks of Nazis and other anti-Semitic groups. The JDL seeks to replace the image of the Jew as weak, frightened, and incapable of fighting back with the image of a Jew who is strong, courageous, and capable of defending him or herself. The JDL is an international organization that advocates violence, if necessary, to protect Jewish people from anti-Semitism.

As you read, consider the following questions:

1. According to the JDL, what is the true solution to the Jewish problem?
2. What is the purpose of anti-Semitic hatred and contempt for Jewish people, in the JDL's opinion?
3. According to the JDL, what will ensure its success?

The Jewish Defense League [JDL] is the most controversial, yet the most effective, of all Jewish organizations. Founded in 1968 by Rabbi Meir Kahane, of blessed memory, the activist group has been responsible for bringing such issues as, but certainly not limited to, Soviet Jewry, Nazi war criminals, Jew-hatred and Jewish self-defense to the front page of every major newspaper. Headquartered in Southern California, JDL devotes its modest resources to the defense of Diaspora Jewish communities and Jewish interests in its own inimitable fashion.

There is no issue facing the Jewish people today that the JDL won't tackle and unlike the so-called "respectable" Jewish establishment organizations the JDL doesn't form committees and study what needs to be done for years on end, thus wasting precious time and accomplishing absolutely nothing! The JDL takes concrete action to solve Jewish problems.

To better understand why JDL does what it does one must read the 5 principles of the JDL to get a better appreciation of our work.

The 5 principles of the JDL are:

Ahavat Yisrael—Love of Jewry

The Jewish Defense League came into being to educate the Jewish people to the concept of Ahavat Yisrael . . . one Jewish people, indivisible and united, from which flows the love for and the feeling of pain of all Jews. It sees the need for a movement that is dedicated specifically to Jewish problems and that allocates its time, resources, energies and funds to Jews. It realizes that in the end . . . with few exceptions . . . the Jew can look to no one but another Jew for help and that the true solution to the Jewish problem is the liquidation of the Exile and the return of all Jews to Eretz Yisrael . . . the land of Israel. It sees the immediate need to place Judaism over any other "ism" and ideology and calls for the use of the yardstick: "Is it good for the Jews?"

Hadar—Dignity and Pride

JDL teaches the concept of Hadar . . . pride in and knowledge of Jewish tradition, faith, culture, land, history, strength, pain and peoplehood. Hadar is the need to have pride in Ju-

Violence Is Sometimes Necessary

The story is told of two Jews being taken out by anti-Semites to be shot. As they were both placed against the wall, blindfolds were placed over their eyes and one cried out: "The blindfold is too tight!"

At which point the other frantically whispered: "Quiet, don't make trouble . . . "

The advertisement appeared in *The New York Times* on June 24, 1969. Over a picture of a group of tough-looking pipe-wielding youngsters was the question:

> Is this any way for a nice Jewish boy to behave?

The question did not wait for an answer. That followed immediately:

> Maybe. Maybe there are times when there is no other way to get across to the extremist that the Jew is not quite the patsy some think he is.
>
> Maybe there is only one way to get across a clear response to people who threaten seizure of synagogues and extortion of money. Maybe nice Jewish boys do not always get through to people who threaten to carry teachers out in pine boxes and burn down merchant's stores.
>
> Maybe some people and organizations are *too* nice. Maybe in times of crisis Jewish boys should not be that nice. Maybe—just maybe—nice people build their own road to Auschwitz.

The text went on to state the problems that had arisen and unorthodox militant solutions to them. It ended with the words: "We are speaking of Jewish survival."

The ad was placed by the Jewish Defense League, which had decided to "make trouble," and after its appearance the Jewish community was never quite the same.

Meir Kahane, *The Story of the Jewish Defense League*, 1975.

---

daism and not allow it to be disgraced and defiled by beating and desecration of Jewish honor. This is the concept that the great Jewish leader Zev Jabotinsky attempted to instill in the oppressed and degraded masses of Eastern Europe during the holocaust over 5 decades ago. The Anti-Semite's hatred and contempt for the Jew is an attempt to degrade us. It is an attempt to instill within the Jew a feeling of inferiority. It is an attempt that all too often succeeds in promoting Jewish self-hatred and shame in an attempt to escape one's Jewishness.

Hadar is pride! Hadar is self-respect! Hadar is dignity in being a Jew!

Barzel—Iron

JDL upholds the principle of Barzel . . . iron . . . the need to both move to help Jews everywhere and to change the Jewish image through sacrifice and through all necessary means . . . even strength, force and violence. The Galut [Diaspora] image of the Jew as a weakling, as one who is easily stepped upon and who does not fight back is an image that must be changed. Not only does that image cause immediate harm to Jews but it is a self-perpetuating thing because if a Jew runs away or because a Jew allows himself to be stepped upon, he guarantees that another Jew in the future will be attacked because of the image he has perpetuated. JDL wants to create a physically strong, fearless and courageous Jew who fights back. We are changing an image born of 2000 years in Galut, an image that must be buried because it has buried us. We train ourselves for the defense of Jewish lives and rights. We learn how to fight physically, for it is better to know how and not have to than have to and not know how.

Mishmaat—Discipline and Unity

Mishmaat . . . discipline and dedication . . . creates within the Jew the knowledge that he (or she) can and will do whatever must be done, and the unity and strength of willpower to bring this into reality. It was the lack of discipline and unity that led continually to the destruction of the Jewish people. It is Jewish unity and self-discipline that will lead to the triumph of the Jewish people.

Bitachon—Faith in G-d and the Indestructability of the Jewish People

Faith in Hashem our G-d and in the greatness of the Jewish people, our Torah, our religion and our land of Israel is Bitachon. It is a faith that is built by our belief in Hashem. . . . The Jewish G-d of Hosts, and the incredible saga of Jewish history that has seen us overcome the flood of enemies that have arisen to wipe us out in every generation. It is this faith in Hashem our G-d and the permanence and survival of the

Jewish people that in turn gives faith to the ultimate success of the Jewish Defense League. No matter how difficult, no matter how impossible the task may seem . . . if it is a good task . . . if it is a holy task . . . it will succeed because it must.

The sources for the philosophy and actions of the Jewish Defense League are Jewish sources. They stem from the wellsprings of Jewish tradition and have their roots in Jewish teachings. In the Torah, the Talmud, in the teachings of our sages throughout the ages in Jewish practice throughout history, the concepts of Ahavat Yisrael, Hadar Yisrael, Barzel Yisrael, Mishmaat Yisrael and Bitachon are hallowed. At the same time an eternal debt is owed to the Jews of our era who also recognized that these concepts are indeed Jewish and who fought the assimilated Jewish tide to put them into practice. We refer to the great Zev Jabotinsky, . . . his followers and his movement of which we consider ourselves to be a spiritual part, and sitting in heaven righteously alongside Jabotinsky is the founder and eternal spiritual leader of the Jewish Defense League, Rabbi Meir Kahane. . . . May the Almighty grant us the understanding to recognize and act on our problems forthrightly and the courage to go out to battle against our enemies in the face of all obstacles . . . from within and without.

> "[The Jewish Defense League is] a racist, terrorist, extremist, militant, Zionist hate group."

The Jewish Defense League Promotes Hate and Violence

Angela Valkyrie

Angela Valkyrie claims in the following viewpoint that the Jewish Defense League (JDL) is an extremist group that promotes hate and violence and whose membership is increasing daily. She maintains that the JDL is a threat to all Americans because members have a victim mentality combined with a superiority complex that leads to criminal behavior motivated by hate and fear. Angela Valkyrie writes for AlterMedia.info, a white supremacist, anti-Semitic Web site.

As you read, consider the following questions:
1. According to Valkyrie, why was Irv Rubin arrested in 1980?
2. Who was the founder of the JDL, in Valkyrie's opinion?
3. What does the author argue was the job of the Chaya Squad?

Angela Valkyrie, "The JDL: Jewish Hate Group," www.altermedia.info, November 24, 2003. Copyright © 2003 by AlterMedia. Reproduced by permission.

There is a Jewish hate group in America. No one in the media seems to want you to know that they exist. But they do exist. And, Altermedia.info USA wants you to know about them. Or more specifically, I want you to know more about them.

This Jewish extremist hate group in America is called the Jewish Defense League (JDL). They claim to have 6,000 members. They are a racist, terrorist, extremist, militant, Zionist hate group. JDL member numbers are growing in the United States every day.

Americans, especially European-Americans need to be aware of the threat the JDL are to us and to the Nation as a whole. Since the mainstream media won't give this topic the attention it deserves, I will.

In December of 2001 in Los Angeles, CA John Gordon of the L.A. U.S. attorney's office announced that two members of the Jewish Defense League had been arrested on conspiracy and terrorist charges. They had been plotting to bomb a mosque in Culver City, CA. The two suspects were identified as Irv Rubin, 56, and Earl Krugel. Irv Rubin had been the National Chairman of the JDL since 1970. This was not the first time that Irv Rubin had been in trouble with the law. Rubin had been arrested at least 50 times on other counts prior to the conspiracy and terrorism charges of December 2001.

As leader of the Jewish Defense League, Rubin had instituted civilian patrols, organized militant programs of firearms and the martial arts.

In 1980, Irv Rubin was known to be soliciting the murders of anyone he considered to be a "Nazi" in the United States. The police charged him with solicitation with murderous intent but then he was acquitted of the charges.

Jewish Defense League Founder

Two of Irv Rubin's favorite JDL slogans were, "I want every Jew, a .22," he has said. "Keep alive with a .45."

The Jewish Defense League was founded in 1968 by well-known Zionist Rabbi Meir Kahane, who left the JDL in 1985 to serve on the Israeli Parliament and then was mysteriously assassinated in 1990.

The Jewish Defense League Promotes Violence

The JDL [Jewish Defense League] was a Jewish self-defense movement that began with the limited goals of protecting orthodox Jewish neighborhoods in New York City from depredations by young black and Puerto Rican hoodlums and to protest local instances of anti-Semitism. Eventually the JDL embraced a universal program of fighting for Jewish interests worldwide. The group was self-sustaining and lacked any support from mainstream Jewish organizations in the United States or from the State of Israel. The JDL was founded in 1968 by Rabbi Meir Kahane, who began to organize young Jewish men as vigilantes to protect Jews and Jewish businesses in the Williamsburg and Crown Heights areas of Brooklyn and elsewhere in the New York City area. Within a year the group had graduated from vigilantism and demonstrations against alleged anti-Semites to burglarizing the files of the [Palestine Liberation Organization United Nations] Mission and launching attacks on Soviet diplomatic, trade, and tourism offices and personnel. According to the FBI, the JDL was responsible for at least 37 terrorist acts in the United States in the period from 1968–1983, while the International Terrorism: Attributes of Terrorist Events (ITERATE) database developed on behalf of the United States Central Intelligence Agency by Edward F. Mickolus recorded 50 such incidents from 1968–1987, making the JDL second only to the Puerto Rican FALN . . . as the major domestic terrorist group. Nonetheless the JDL is a legally incorporated political action group and has officially disavowed responsibility for any violent actions carried out by its members. Bombings accounted for 78 percent of all JDL terrorist activities; shootings accounted for 16 percent; while arson attacks, vandalism, kidnapping, threats, and verbal harassment accounted for the rest.

Sean Anderson and Stephan Sloan, *Historical Dictionary of Terrorism*, 1995.

It was Kahane who originally coined the popular JDL slogan, "every Jew a .22." He created the Kahane's Chaya Squad, a group within the JDL, whose job was to, and I quote, "instill fear in the hearts of the would-be criminals against Jews" according to Rabbi Meir Kahane. He adamantly spoke out against the intermarriage of Jews and the importance of maintaining the purity of the Jewish race.

Kahane was jailed many times for breaking the law in JDL related militant activities and was sentenced to prison before he finally decided to move his operations to Israel.

Kach Movement

After Kahane immigrated to Israel he formed the Kach movement.

The Kach movement was most famous for its platform calling for the removal of the the entire Israeli-Arab population from Israel and transferring them "elsewhere." The Kach movement under Rabbi Kahane demanded the demolition and complete annihilation of all Palestinian territories followed by unlimited Jewish-Israeli settlement and the complete and final colonization of Palestine.

Rabbi Kahane considered Israel to be the chosen nation by G-d and the exclusive owners of the Holy Land. He was a self-confirmed Zionist who loathed American Democracy. He is quoted here as having said, "Judaism is not Thomas Jefferson and the Middle East is not the Midwest.". . .

Terrorist Activities

So now you are a bit more informed about the Jewish Defense League than you were before. Now you know what the media does not want you to know.

In closing, I give you a short compiled list summarizing a few JDL activities to look over:

- The 1985 murder of Alex Odeh, director of the American Arab Anti-Discrimination Committee.
- Terrorist bombings.
- Plotting to bomb a mosque in Culver City, CA in December of 2001.
- Conspiracy and terrorism charges.
- Organized militant programs of firearms and the martial arts.
- Solicitation with murderous intent.
- Ties with Mossad, the Israeli Zionist militant extremist group.
- Explosives and stockpiled weaponry.
- Blatant hatred towards Christians, Arab-Americans, Muslims, Blacks and European-Americans. . . .
- Training Jewish children to use guns and martial arts.
- JDL slogans like; "I want every Jew, a .22" and "Keep alive with a .45."
- Mysterious assassinations.

- Convicted felons owning and handling firearms.
- Website advertising weapons courses at Camp Jabotinsky.
- Stirring up hatred by faking "anti-Semitic" activity.
- Twisting the truth and using it as propaganda.
- The JDL belief that intermarriage is forbidden because Jews must perpetuate the Jewish race by having children who are not only religiously Jewish but ethnically Jewish.
- Whole-heartedly dedicating their lives to fighting a holy war using violence, intimidation tactics and murder.
- Victim mentality scapegoating combined with a superiority complex that leads to self-righteous criminal behavior motivated by hate and fear.

With all that read, is the JDL a terrorist hate group? Decide for yourself.

Periodical Bibliography

The following articles have been selected to supplement the diverse views presented in this chapter.

Chuck Baldwin	"Is America Losing Her Purpose? God Raised America to Preach Gospel, Protect Israel, Preserve Liberty," *Free Republic*, October 5, 2001.
James Dobson	"The New Cost of Discipleship," *Christianity Today*, September 6, 1999.
Amy Driscoll	"Religious Right Sees New Hope for Morality Agenda," *Miami Herald*, February 22, 1999.
Jonah Goldberg	"Jewish Defense League Plotters Are Terrorists," TownHall.com, December 14, 2001.
Delinda C. Hanley	"Freeze on Jewish Defense League Assets Called for After JDL Bomb Plot Failed," *Washington Report on Middle East Affairs*, January/February 2002.
John Hicks	"The Political Substance of the Religious Right: Why the Christian Right Survives and Does Not Thrive," The American Religious Experience, 2000. http://are.as.wvu.edu.
Jewish Defense League	"The Five Principles of the Jewish Defense League," 1999. www.jdl.org.
Ruqaiyyah Waris Maqsood	"On the Hijacking of Islam," Islam for Today, September 16, 2001. www.islamfortoday.com.
Steven E. Miller	"The New Right Wing Agenda," Common Dreams, June 13, 2003. www.commondreams.org.
Carroll Payne	"What Is Islam?" *World Conflict Quarterly*, October 2001. www.globalterrorism101.com.
Daniel Pipes	"Aim the War on Terror at Militant Islam," *Los Angeles Times*, January 6, 2002.
Daniel Pipes	"Protecting Muslims While Rooting Out Islamists," *Daily Telegraph* (London), September 14, 2001.
Laura Montgomery Rutt	"H.R. 2357—Religious Right's Newest Attempt to Destroy Democracy," *Progressive Voices*, Winter 2001.
Unitarian Universalist Association	"The Religious Right's Agenda for 1999 and Beyond," July 29, 1999. www.uua.org.
Westchester Coalition for Legal Abortion	"Barry Lynn: Educate Public About Religious Right Agenda," Spring 1999. www.wcla.org.

CHAPTER 2

Do Some Liberal Groups Benefit Society?

Chapter Preface

Some radical animal rights organizations such as the Animal Liberation Front (ALF) and People for the Ethical Treatment of Animals (PETA) engage in violent acts of destruction and vandalism in an effort to stop what they perceive to be the cruel exploitation of animals. Other animal rights advocacy groups such as the Animal Legal Defense Fund (ALDF) have taken a less violent—though no less radical—approach to securing the rights of animals. The ALDF is working to achieve legal status in court for all animals. By fundamentally changing their legal status, ALDF hopes to put an end to the exploitation of animals, particularly the use of animals as research subjects. Steve Ann Chambers, president of the ALDF insists, "We need to expand legal rights beyond humans." The ALDF claims that changing the legal status of animals will result in far-reaching moral, ethical, and environmental benefits to society.

The ALDF is not alone in its fight for animal rights. Twenty-five U.S. law schools now offer courses in animal rights (in the mid-1990s, there were only five offering such courses). University of Chicago professor Cass Sunstein argues that although animals are regarded as property, they can still have rights under the law and that there is significant popular support for such changes. Sunstein said, "Our culture is much more interested in protecting animals than our laws are." Steven Wise, author of *Rattling the Cage: Toward Legal Rights for Animals*, maintains that nonhuman animals, particularly primates, "have a kind of autonomy that judges should easily recognize as sufficient for legal rights." While some progress is being made, the fight for animal rights is likely to be a long one.

Some radical animal rights activist groups such as the ALDF are working to end the exploitation of animals without resorting to violence but nevertheless using what many would call extreme means. Authors in the following chapter explore the issues raised by radical animal rights activists and other extremist groups.

"The healthiest generation in history is a ripe target for the anti-science nonsense pushed by the animal rights movement."

Radical Animal Rights Groups Harm Society

Frederick K. Goodwin and Adrian R. Morrison

Radical animal rights activists misguidedly harass scientists and disrupt research critical to human and animal welfare, argue Fredrick K. Goodwin and Adrian R. Morrison in the following viewpoint. The authors maintain that even though scientists and research facilities follow the strictest animal care guidelines, they are targets of violent attacks that inspire fear among researchers and stifle scientific creativity. Frederick K. Goodwin is a former director of the National Institute of Mental Health. Adrian R. Morrison is a professor of veterinary medicine at the University of Pennsylvania.

As you read, consider the following questions:

1. According to the authors, what is the difference between the animal rights movement and animal welfare organizations?
2. Name one of the factors that Goodwin and Morrison identify as contributing to the climate of moral confusion surrounding the use of animals in research.
3. In the authors' opinion, what was the disastrous tactical error that scientists made at the outset of their encounter with the animal rights movement?

Frederick K. Goodwin and Adrian R. Morrison, "Science and Self-Doubt," *Reason*, vol. 32, October 2000, p. 22. Copyright © 2000 by the Reason Foundation, 3415 S. Sepulveda Blvd., Suite 400, Los Angeles, CA 90034, www.reason.com. Reproduced with permission.

Twenty years ago, animal research became the target of a new generation of anti-vivisectionists: the radical "animal rights" movement. That movement, which views animals as moral agents on a par with people, has promoted a profoundly confused philosophy that equates animal research with the enslavement of human beings.

Scientists responded to this movement by proposing to strengthen the standards and regulation of animal research and care. But even as the handling of research animals became ever more restricted, the animal rights campaign became ever more demanding and violent. Scientists working with animals, especially those involved in brain and behavioral research, were assaulted in their laboratories, harassed in their homes, and threatened with death.

In Europe, scientists have long been the target of actual terrorism, now identified as such by the United Kingdom. Indeed, the neuroscientist Colin Blakemore at Oxford University, who studies brain activity in cats, literally lives under siege. Police must protect his home, which has been assaulted with his frightened wife and daughters in residence. Why? He spoke out in support of the obvious necessity of using animals to advance medical science—to alleviate the suffering of human beings—and has been in danger ever since that principled act. In 1998, Blakemore and other European scientists were marked for death by animal rights terrorists, and Blakemore lived for months under round-the-clock police protection.

The United States Is the Latest Target

Although for a few years American researchers enjoyed relative peace, animal rights activists struck last spring [2000] at the University of Minnesota, causing thousands of dollars in damage. A scientist studying hearing at the University of California at San Francisco is now suffering what Blakemore has endured for years. But biomedical research is coming under another kind of siege.

There has been a campaign in New Zealand to give the great apes constitutional rights, an outgrowth of the ideas of the animal rights movement and the Great Ape Project, which seeks to award apes the same rights as those possessed by humans. Last year [1999] in Germany, the ruling Social Democratic and Green parties introduced legislation stating that animals have the right to be "respected as fellow creatures," and to be protected from "avoidable pain." Two recent developments in the United States suggest that we may be entering a dangerous era in thinking about animals.

In the first, a U.S. court recognized the legal standing of an individual to sue the federal government in order to force changes in animal-welfare regulations. In that case, the individual claimed "harm" as a result of seeing animals mistreated, in his opinion, at a roadside zoo; the plaintiff held the Department of Agriculture [USDA] responsible. However, in deciding the merits of the case, an appeals court later found that USDA was not responsible for the individual's alleged harm, and declined to order any change in the current regulations.

In the second, animal rights groups are pushing USDA to include rats and mice under the Animal Welfare Act.

Animal Rights Versus Animal Welfare

The campaign to end the use of animals in biomedical research is based upon a complete misunderstanding of how scientists work, what research requires, and what has made possible our era's outpouring of lifesaving advances in medicine. Unfortunately, neither their misunderstanding of science nor their misguided philosophy has prevented activists from becoming an increasingly powerful, militant force—one now threatening the discovery of new medical treatments and preventive strategies for serious illnesses.

To understand the animal rights movement, we must distinguish its objectives from those of animal welfare organizations. Typically, such organizations as local societies for the prevention of cruelty to animals will care for strays, teach good animal care, run neutering programs, and build animal shelters. Acting as the stewards of animals, especially those not in a position to care for themselves, these organizations uphold our traditional values of humane, caring treatment of sentient creatures.

Animal rights organizations, on the other hand, invest their energies in campaigning against various uses of animals, including research. They start with a completely different philosophy, summed up by Peter Singer, the acknowledged founder of the animal rights movement, in his 1975 book, *Animal Liberation*. Singer, now De Camp Professor of Bioethics at Princeton University, argues that sentient creatures—all those capable of feeling pain—must essentially be considered moral equivalents to human beings, certainly as equivalent to the severely brain-damaged and to human infants before the age of reasoning. Anyone who dismisses any sentient creature as merely an animal to be used for human benefit is guilty of "speciesism," a prejudice morally equivalent to racism and sexism. (Singer, who is Australian, does not base his opposition to animal research on the concept of rights; his American counterpart, University of North Carolina philosophy professor Tom Regan, does.)

PETA

On the political front, Ingrid Newkirk, the national director of People for the Ethical Treatment of Animals (PETA), asserted in 1983 that "animal liberationists do not separate out the human animal, so there is no rational basis for saying that a human being has special rights. A rat is a pig is a dog is a boy. They're all mammals." She has also said, "Six million Jews died in concentration camps, but six billion broiler chickens will die this year in slaughterhouses." Chris DeRose, who heads an organization called In Defense of Animals, said recently that even if the death of one rat would cure all disease, that death still would not be right, because we are all equal.

Despite PETA's view that broiler chickens are the moral equivalent of murdered Jews, animal rights activists decided early on to target scientific researchers, not farmers, although more than 99 percent of the animals used by people are for food (or clothing, or killed either in pounds or by hunters) and just a fraction of 1 percent for research. Singer has said that the strategic decision to level protests against science was made because farmers are organized and politically powerful (and live in rural areas, which makes them hard to get at). In contrast, scientists are not politically organized, live in urban areas, and can be hard put to explain their work in lay language.

Neuroscientists have been a frequent target. Two key fields of neuroscience, behavioral and addiction research, were highlighted in Singer's book. High-profile laboratory invasions have targeted scientists engaged in brain research. For example, PETA, which adheres to Singer's philosophy, established itself by infiltrating the laboratory of neuroscientist Edward Taub in Silver Spring, Maryland, in 1981, and "exposing" deficient laboratory conditions with photographs that purported to show animal mistreatment. Taub, however, has noted that no one else in the lab observed the conditions in the PETA photographs, and he is supported by the sworn statements of seven people, including a USDA inspector, who testified at Taub's subsequent trial. At the time, Taub was investigating how monkeys perform complex tasks with certain nerve pathways in their arms severed, work that was the basis for the subsequent development of improved methods for stroke rehabilitation.

In 1984, PETA exploited the Animal Liberation Front's invasion of the University of Pennsylvania Head Injury Research Laboratory by cleverly editing videotapes taken in the raid and using the resulting composite as a fund raising tool. In subsequent literature, PETA made it clear that alleged mistreatment of animals was not the real issue. In PETA's view, animals cannot be used to alleviate health problems of people, period. Even after more stringent government controls over animal research were in place (by 1985) Texas Tech sleep researcher John Orem suffered a raid in 1989 that resulted in $40,000 worth of damage to his laboratory. In this and other cases, however, the critical damage is to the scientist's will to continue research.

Moral Confusion

Many factors have contributed to the climate of moral confusion surrounding the use of animals in research and to the apparent willingness of many people to credit the bizarre ideas of the animal rights activists.

For one thing, we are victims of our own health care successes. We have enjoyed such a victory over infectious diseases that baby boomers and subsequent generations do not even remember polio and other dreaded infectious diseases, and have little sense of how amazing it was when antibiotics were first developed. With the eradication of so many deadly infectious diseases, antibiotics have become something that you take for incidental minor infection. The healthiest generation in history is a ripe target for the anti-science nonsense pushed by the animal rights movement.

Second, America has sustained a steady, devastating decline in scientific literacy. Our high school students consistently rank below those of other developed countries. As a result, most people, especially young people, do not understand what the scientific method is really about.

Asay. © by Charles Asay. Reproduced by permission.

Additionally, Americans today spend little time around animals other than house pets. It is worth remembering that just before World War II one in four of us lived on a farm; now it is one in 50. What do most urban and suburban kids know about animals, other than what they see in cartoons?

Such factors have helped propel the ever-tightening regulation of research, stifling the creativity that is its essence and posing a threat to the human well-being that is its goal. Many major discoveries in the history of medicine have come about by serendipity, when a scientist has had his sights trained on an entirely different topic of research. The story behind the initial discovery that lithium, an elemental substance on the periodic table, might have therapeutic benefits illustrates this serendipity and demonstrates how basic research with animals can lead to major medical advances.

In that case, Australian psychiatrist John Cade asked what might be wrong in the brains of patients with manic-depressive illness and wondered whether a substance called urea would have therapeutic value. Testing his hypothesis on guinea pigs, Cade gave them a salt form of urea, which happened to contain lithium. The guinea pigs became unexpectedly calm. Further experimentation revealed that the urea had nothing to do with this result; it was caused by the lithium—a complete surprise to Cade. Having laid his foundation with animal research, Cade extended his findings by giving lithium to manic patients, who experienced an alleviation of their manic excitement without being sedated. This single discovery has revolutionized treatment of manic-depressive illness, easing the lives of millions and saving billions of dollars along the way. At the same time, it has opened whole new productive areas for brain research.

No one could have predicted the outcome of Cade's initial experiment with urea. There was no way to list in advance what the health benefits of using guinea pigs would be. That would have required knowing the answer to a question that had not yet been asked. If one already knows the answer, research is unnecessary.

Few Studies Involve Animals

In 1976, before the animal rights controversy arose, the National Institutes of Health sponsored a study by Julius H. Comroe Jr. and R.D. Dripps to ascertain if government funding of basic biomedical research had been a good investment. The authors asked practicing cardiologists what they regarded as the 10 leading medical advances of their lifetimes; the scientists named such advances as cardiac surgery, drug treatment of hypertension, and medical treatment of cardiac insufficiency. Comroe and Dripps then traced the scientific ancestry of each of these discoveries and found that 40 percent of the studies leading to the advances originated from work in a different, seemingly unrelated field of research. Animal research was fundamental to many of these studies. Regulations that require justification of animal research in terms of its specific outcomes, rather than the clarity of the hypotheses and strength of the research design, may end much of the creative research now under way.

Less than a quarter of the studies in biomedicine involve animals (and more than 90 percent of those are rats and mice), but anyone working in the field will tell you that such animal studies are indispensable. One cannot develop an understanding of a chemical or a gene, then try to ascertain its role in a complex human organism with billions of cells and dozens of organs, without first knowing how it works in the biological systems of animals. The animal model enables a scientist to understand what is happening at a level of detail that could not be reached in humans.

The great kidney transplant pioneer Dr. Thomas E. Starzl was once asked why he used dogs in his work. He explained that, in his first series of operations, he had transplanted kidneys into a number of subjects, and that the majority of them died. After figuring out what had enabled a few to survive, he revised his techniques and operated on a similar group of subjects; a majority of them survived. In his third group of subjects, only one or two died, and in his fourth group all survived. The important point, said Starzl, was that the first three groups of subjects were dogs; the fourth group consisted of human babies. Had Starzl begun his series of experimental operations on people, he would have killed at least 15 people. Yet there are activists who believe, in the name of animal rights, that that is what Starzl should have done.

At the outset of their encounter with the animal rights movement, scientists made a disastrous tactical error. Accustomed to dealing with others by reason, and eager to meet the activists halfway, the research community adopted "The Three Rs," described as long ago as 1959 by W. Russell and R. Birch in their book, *The Principles of Humane Experimental Technique*. Scientists pledged to reduce the number of animals used, to refine their techniques, and to replace animals whenever possible. In truth, scientists are always looking for ways to reduce, refine, and replace animal use. It makes sense from the point of view of humane treatment, the economics of research and, often, science.

But this response came across as a confession of guilt. Although scientists accept high standards for the use and care of research animals, they are not engaged in some kind of "necessary evil." Appeasement is a losing game. To make concessions on a matter of principle is to concede the principle itself. Then defeat is only a matter of time, as opponents demand complete consistency with their own principle.

Rights Are a Human Concept

"Rights," the idea that the activists are working so hard to enlist in their cause, are a moral concept. Rights stem from the uniquely human capacity to choose values and principles, then act on choices and judgment. Within that context, rights are moral principles stating that, as human beings with the ability to develop and act on moral judgments, we must leave each other free to do so. That is the basis of our claim to political and personal freedom. Rattlesnakes and rats, tigers and sheep, and even our closest animal relatives, chimpanzees, exhibit no ability to comprehend, respect, or act upon rights. The "law of the jungle" is no law at all. Indeed, the concept of rights is profoundly incoherent when applied to animals. It is worse than mistaken; it dangerously subverts the concept of rights itself at a time when human rights worldwide are in need of clear articulation and defense.

Focusing on the Three Rs without exposing and refuting the underlying philosophy of animal rights proved a public relations catastrophe. The research community's basic position should have been that human beings have a right to use animals for human purposes, but also have a responsibility to use animals humanely. The more we emphasized the Three Rs, the stronger the animal rights movement became, and the more money the radical activists raised. This was occurring at the very same time that science was demonstrating noticeable improvements in the handling of laboratory animals.

It is not sufficient for the medical-scientific community to expose the fundamental flaws in the philosophy of animal rights. It must be able to respond to the movement's other, more utilitarian, arguments against the use of animals in research.

Activists' Arguments Are Weak

Activists assert that animal research is cruel. But their argument misses the point that experimenters usually want to disturb the animal as little as possible, since their goal is to study its natural response to whatever is being tested. An estimated 7 percent of research does employ procedures causing pain in order to understand pain mechanisms in the central nervous system. This kind of experimentation has enabled us to develop effective painkillers.

Activists claim that animal experiments are duplicative. The reality is that today only one out of four grant requests is funded, a highly competitive situation that makes duplicative research scarce. But research does have to be replicated before the results are accepted; and progress usually arises from a series of small discoveries, all elaborating on or overlapping one another. When activists talk about duplication, they betray a fundamental misunderstanding of how science progresses. Nor do they understand scientists. What highly trained, creative individual wants to do exactly what someone has already done?

Activists urge prevention rather than treatment. They say we should urge people to adopt measures such as an altered diet or increased exercise to prevent major illness, so that we would not need so many new treatments. But much of what we have discovered about preventive measures has itself resulted from animal research. You cannot get most cancers to grow in a test tube; you need whole animal studies.

Activists argue that we should use alternatives to animal research. A favorite example is computer simulations. But where do they think the data that are entered into computers come from? To get real answers, one has to feed computers real physiological data. There is an argument that researchers should use PET scans, which can provide an image of how a living human organ is functioning, as a way of avoiding the use of animals. It took Lou Sokoloff at the National Institute of Mental Health eight years of animal research to develop the PET scan methodology. . . .

Moral Self-Doubt

We live in an age of moral self-doubt. Some scientists and other individuals associated with biomedical research in supportive roles have begun to feel guilt over their use of animals. That has spawned a group calling itself the "troubled middle" (a rather presumptuous phrase, suggesting that only they care about the issues raised by animal research). Indeed, a whole industry has grown up around this sense of guilt, with constant, somewhat repetitive conferences focusing on how to oversee research, how to be the perfect member of an Institutional Animal Care and Use Committee, and how to find alternatives to using animals. These topics are not unworthy, but the conferences give short shrift to the perspectives of working scientists, who rarely appear as major speakers.

Progress toward increased human well-being cannot flourish amid such self-doubt. Scientists and members of the public who support their work must recognize that they are engaged in a struggle for minds. Their own minds therefore must be clear about what justifies animal research when necessary: that human beings are special. Researchers and others must appreciate the value of such work, and must be ready to state unequivocally and publicly that human life comes first. We who work with animals, and those who support the benefits of that work, have made a moral choice, and we must be willing to stand by it.

"By performing illegal actions the Band [of Mercy] was able to directly save the lives of animals by destroying the tool of torture and death."

Radical Animal Activism Is Justified

Noel Molland

In the following viewpoint Noel Molland maintains that radical animal activism is justified because conventional legal methods do not bring about desired changes in people's thinking or behavior toward animals. He insists that saving animal lives is as important as saving human lives. Molland claims that destroying property and frightening people is often the most effective way to make the public understand the revolutionary nature of the animal rights movement. Noel Molland is a contributor to *No Compromise*, the publication of No Compromise, a direct action animal liberation organization.

As you read, consider the following questions:
1. According to Molland, what group did John Prestidge found in 1964?
2. Why was the Band of Mercy formed, in the author's opinion?
3. Why does Molland argue that the Hoechst Pharmaceutical building had to be destroyed?

I t is hard, if not impossible, to say when the Animal/Earth Liberation movement first started. A study of the subject literally takes you back thousands of years to 200 B.C. when people like Pythagoras advocated vegetarianism & animal compassion on spiritual grounds, and to the 1st century A.D. when Plutarch wrote what is widely regarded as the first animal rights literature.

However, the reader will be delighted to know that I am not going to bore you to death with 2000 years of waffle. Instead, I merely intend to look at what occurred 30 years ago this year [2002]. But first, to fully understand the events of 30 years ago, we must look slightly further back than that, to the events of 1964.

During the 19th and 20th centuries Britain saw a wealth of Animal Welfare and Rights groups established. However, these groups by and large relied upon the parliamentary way of legal reform to achieve their aims. This process was incredibly slow and achievements were minor. Even the 1911 Animal Protection Act treated animals as property and offered no protection to wild-born creatures. By the mid-nineteen sixties people started to look around for other ways of campaigning and in 1964 John Prestidge found that new style.

The Hunt Saboteurs Association

In 1964 in Brixham, Devon, England, John Prestidge founded a group that would actively oppose blood sports. Rather than campaigning for parliamentary reforms, John's new group was prepared to directly go out into the fields of Britain and do everything they could, within the law, to prevent the killing of British wildlife: John founded the Hunt Saboteurs Association (H.S.A.).

The popularity of this new form of campaigning was instant. Just a year after the H.S.A. was founded, hunt saboteur groups were active across the English Westcountry in Devon, Somerset and Bristol. Groups also started to emerge outside of the Westcountry in places like Birmingham, Hampshire and Surrey.

Originally a single Devon-based group, the H.S.A. soon became a national network of dedicated activists using lawful methods to disrupt blood-junkies of Britain and to prevent the "green and pleasant lands" from literally becoming the killing fields.

And so it was, in 1971, as part of the ever-expanding H.S.A. network, a new hunt sab [saboteurs] group was formed in Luton. The group was founded by a law student named Ronnie Lee. The Luton hunt sabs, like a lot of other hunt sab groups, soon became very successful in saving the lives of animals. Many a hunt soon found their sadistic day's entertainment ruined by the Luton Gang.

However, despite the success of the Luton hunt sabs in the field, it soon became apparent to some people within the groups that the strictly legal actions of the H.S.A. could only ever go so far to preventing animal suffering. The problem was that if a hunt is allowed to be active, no matter how good a hunt sab group may be, there is a chance that an animal may be harmed or killed.

Even if the sabs do manage to prevent an animal from being killed, the fear the animal goes through whilst being hunted is tremendous. Contemporary vet reports, gathered at the end of the 20th century, have revealed animals do suffer incredible stress whilst being hunted.

The Hunt Must Never Begin

It was out of this recognition (that strictly legal hunt sabotage couldn't totally prevent the suffering of an animal) that Ronnie Lee and a few close friends started to look around for other ways to help prevent suffering. They realized that the only real way to prevent any sort of suffering is to assure that the hunt is never allowed to become active in the first place. As soon as an animal is being chased, she is psychologically suffering as she fears for her life. Therefore she has to be assured that 'the chase' is never allowed to start in the first place. With this aim in mind, Ronnie Lee, Cliff Goodman and possibly two or three other people, decided to form the Band of Mercy in 1972.

The name the Band of Mercy was chosen because it had been the name of an earlier animal liberation direct action group. During the 19th century, an anti-slavery activist named Catherine Smithies had set up a youth wing to the RSPCA [Royal Society for the Prevention of Cruelty to Animals] called the Bands of Mercy. By and large these youth groups were just normal young supporters of the RSPCA who told stories of heroic animal deeds and who took oaths of compassion to the animals. However some of these young Victorian animal rights activists were a little more zealous than others and went around sabotaging hunting rifles. The activities of the Victorian Bands of Mercy became so great that there was even a theatrical play written during which a group of children sabotages a hunting rifle.

For Ronnie Lee and his companions the Victorian Bands of Mercy were a fine example of direct action, so they decided to adopt their not-strictly-legal approach to saving lives.

Initially, the Band of Mercy concentrated on small actions directed against the hunt during the cub-hunting season. Cub hunting is when young hounds are taught to tear young fox cubs apart in order for the hound to get the taste for killing.

The initial actions of the Band of Mercy were very simple and were basically designed around the idea of disabling the hunt vehicles in order to slow down or even stop the hunt from carrying out its murderous activities.

However, the Band of Mercy was very clear from the beginning that it was not merely carrying out acts of wanton vandalism against those whom they opposed but instead their actions were designed around the idea of 'active compassion'. To this aim the Band would always leave a message to the hunters explaining why the Band had carried out their actions, the logic of animal liberation and to show that there was nothing personal against any one individual person.

Illegal Direct Action

The success of the Band of Mercy was soon clear. By carrying out illegal direct action, the Band was able to prevent the hunts. By preventing the hunts from ever becoming active, the Band was safe in the knowledge that not only have they saved the lives of innocent animals, but they had also prevented the psychological suffering of 'the chase'.

Recognizing their true potential for the prevention of animal suffering, the Band then started to think about ways to expand and develop their campaigns. Following on from their early successes the Band soon became much more daring. Towards the end of 1973, the Band learnt about the construction of a new vivisection laboratory. The research laboratory was being built near Milton Keynes for a company called Hoechst Pharmaceutical.

Breaking the Law Is Not Inappropriate

The overall attempt at creating any type of change, socially or politically, should be looked at as a puzzle, because just like a puzzle we need certain pieces to come together and become whole in order to be successful. Specific to animal liberation, we need those out there spreading the word about animal suffering and clueing the general public in on the vegan lifestyle, to create an overall consciousness. We need those on the legal front enforcing the acknowledgment of animals within the law and looking to ban such inhumane, legal events and practices such as the circus and racing, fur trapping and farming. Amongst the other puzzle pieces that I've neglected to mention as examples of necessary pieces in order for the proper connections to be made that will bring about change and bring this movement to success is directly acting on behalf of the animals or yes, breaking the law. We need those out there breaking the law to bring immediate attention to an extreme situation. We need to present that the extreme situation that the animals are in, does call for extreme measures to be taken on their behalf.

I feel that breaking the law should not be looked at as inappropriate even though it may be seen as such by the vast majority. Those willing to take a stand as the voice for the voiceless, those who value life over property, should look at the concept of breaking the law as secondary to the action itself. What can be accomplished and the necessary aspect of the action itself is what is primary. The fact that a law enacted by the state will be broken posing possible consequences should merely serve as the risk involved when taking such actions.

"Interview with Animal Rights Activist, Peter Schnell," *Liberation Magazine*, April 4, 2003.

Having learnt about its existence, two of the Band's activists visited the vivisection lab building site a few times whilst trying to decide the best course of action to be taken. Together these activists realized that if they could prevent the building from ever being completed, then they could prevent the suffering of animals destined to be tortured within its four walls. The Band had to assure the construction could never be finished and eventually decided that the best way to destroy the construction was through the use of arson.

By destroying the building, the Band would prevent the vivisectors from ever being able to start their brand of sadistic 'science'. And even if the damage caused by the fire could be repaired, the restoration work would all cost money that would have to be paid for by Hoechst Pharmaceutical (thus meaning less money to spend on torturing animals).

On November 10th, 1973, the Band of Mercy conducted its first ever action against the vivisection industry. Two activists gained access into the half completed building at Milton Keynes. Once inside the activists set fire to the building. This action was a double watershed for the movement as it was not only the Band's first action against the vivisection industry; it was also the Band's first use of arson.

In that first fire an amazing £26,000 worth of damage was caused. More incredible was six days later, the Band of Mercy returned and started another fire in the same building causing a further £20,000 damage.

To make sure everyone knew why the building was set alight, the Band of Mercy sent a message to the press. The statement read:

"The building was set fire to in an effort to prevent the torture and murder of our animal brothers and sisters by evil experiments. We are a non-violent guerrilla organization dedicated to the liberation of animals from all forms of cruelty and persecution at the hands of mankind. Our actions will continue until our aims are achieved".

After the Milton Keynes arson, the next major action occurred in June 1974 when the Band turned its attention to the bloody seal cull of the Wash along the Norfolk coast.

Stopping the Seal Cull

The seal cull was an annual event and involved hunters going out in two Home Office licensed boats and butchering seals. Seal culling is a bloody attack and the seal has no hope of escape. Knowing how sick the seal cull is the Band obviously wanted to prevent the cull from ever starting. With the goal of preventing the cull from ever starting and regarding the success in the use of arson in the November

1973 action, the Band once again decided to use arson as a campaign tool to destroy the tools of animal murder.

In June 1974 the Band of Mercy set out [on] their second major action. Under the cover of darkness, two activists sought out the Home Office licensed boats. Having found the boats, these transporters of death were then set alight. One of the boats was sadly only slightly damaged by the fire; the other however, was totally destroyed.

After conducting this June 1974 action, the Band of Mercy decided that this time they wouldn't leave a message claiming responsibility. Instead they wanted to leave the sealers wondering what on earth had happened, if those responsible would return and if someone else provided two new boats, if these new vessels would meet with the same fiery fate.

That year there was no seal cull at all due to the actions of the Band of Mercy. Also, besides totally halting the seal cull for that year, there was another knock on effect. Because of the fire, the owner of the two Home Office licensed boats went out of business. And having seen one person's business totally destroyed by the actions of these anonymous arsonists, no one was keen to invest the money into a new business that might very well go the same way. Because of this fear no one has ever attempted to re-start a seal culling business and there has never been a seal cull at the Wash since. Because of the actions of two activists, countless numbers of seals have been saved from the bloody annual seal cull.

Looking back on the June 1974 action it is clear for everyone to see that what happened was an amazing success. Not only were de facto seals saved at the time, but generations of seals to come have also been saved from the seal cullers. Sadly, however, despite the fact the Band of Mercy was saving lives and preventing suffering, not everyone in the animal liberation movement approved of their tactics.

In July 1974 a member of the Hunt Saboteurs Association offered a reward of £250 for information that would inform upon the Band of Mercy. Speaking on behalf of the local sab group the person represented, the spokesperson told the press, "We approve of their ideals, but are opposed to their methods."

How anyone can say they approve of a person's ideals and then side against them by offering a reward for their capture is a total mystery. Fortunately, despite this act of treachery, the Band of Mercy had by now realized its power. By performing illegal actions the Band was able to directly save the lives of animals by destroying the tool of torture and death. Even if the weaker members of the movement rejected the Band's ideas, the Band realized its work had to continue. To stop would be to let the animals down.

The First Animal Rescue

Following the anti-seal action the Band of Mercy then launched its first intensive wave of campaigning against the vivisection industry. In the months leading up to the action at the Wash, the Band of Mercy had been able to gather some inside information about vivisection laboratory animal suppliers. All of this information was gathered and stored, waiting for the day it could be used to its fullest effect. And so it was, that following the action at the Wash, the Band was able to launch straight into a wave of actions against the vivisection industry.

Between June and August 1974 the Band of Mercy launched eight raids against vivisection lab animal suppliers. The main emphasis of the actions was to cause economic sabotage by either damaging buildings or vehicles. But the Band also reached another landmark in their history by carrying out their first-ever animal rescue during this period.

The first Band of Mercy animal rescue happened in Wiltshire in the English Westcountry. A guinea pig farm was targeted and the activists managed to rescue half a dozen of the inmates. Besides being a landmark action for being the first Band of Mercy animal rescue, the action also produced an unexpected but very welcome outcome. The guinea pig farm owner was so shaken by the raid she began to fear that more activists would turn up during the night. With such a fear of the masked strangers breaking into her home, this uncaring capitalist who profited from animal torture took the only course of sensible action: she closed her business.

Besides targeting the vivisection industry, the Band of Mercy also continued to take actions against the hunt. But not wanting to limit their actions to just two forms of animal abuse, the Band also targeted chicken breeders and the firearm lobby. In July 1974, a gun shop in Marlborough was attacked and damaged. The original Victorian Bands of Mercy could surely be proud that their great deeds were being continued in a twentieth-century form.

For a small group of friends, consisting of less than half a dozen activists, the Band of Mercy was able to make a tremendous impact against the animal abusers and their presence was truly felt. Sadly, however, the Band of Mercy's luck ran out in August 1974.

In August 1974 the Band of Mercy targeted Oxford Laboratory Animal Colonies in Bicester. The first action was a success. But then the Band of Mercy made the mistake of returning to O.L.A.C. two days later (I should point out its very easy with hindsight to say it was a mistake to return, but back then it was a perfectly logical action). It was on this second raid the activists, Ronnie Lee and Cliff Goodman, were spotted by a security guard. After being spotted the police were called and Ronnie and Cliff were promptly arrested.

If the police had hoped that the arrests would bring an end to the Band of Mercy, they were very mistaken. The arrest of Ronnie Lee and Cliff Goodman gave a fresh wave of publicity to the Band of Mercy. Rather than being regarded as terrorists, many people viewed the Band as heroes. These two young men were seen as a sort of latter day Robin Hood for the animals. Ronnie and Cliff were soon canonized as the Bicester Two. Throughout the hearing daily demonstrations took place outside the court. Support for the Bicester Two was very strong and came from the most unlikely of quarters. Even Ronnie Lee's local Member of Parliament, the Free Church Minister Ivor Clemitson, joined in the campaign for their release.

Strong Public Support

Despite the strong public support for the Bicester Two, both Ronnie Lee and Cliff Goodman were given three years imprisonment. A letter published in the *Daily Telegraph* shows the anger felt at the outcome of the first animal liberation trial.

"Many would sympathize with their action against the utterly diabolical and largely unnecessary form of cruelty involved in animal experimentation. These young men, while defying the law, showed great courage, and the sentences of three years imprisonment seems unrealistic and harsh."

Now, it is said you can't keep a good Animal/Earth liberation activist down. This is certainly true in the case of Ronnie Lee. After the sentencing, Ronnie and Cliff split up. Ronnie was moved to Winchester prison and Cliff went back to Oxford prison (whilst on remand [awaiting trial] both Ronnie and Cliff were inmates of Oxford prison).

At Winchester prison Ronnie discovered that provisions for vegans in prison were less than desirable. So once at Winchester, to try and assure a decent meal and proper vegan clothing Ronnie went on a hunger strike. This hunger strike gained a great deal of media attention and once again the issue of animal liberation was being openly discussed. With the spotlight once again being focused on animal liberation Ronnie soon expanded his hunger strike demands to include issues revolving around Porton Down, the Government's chemical and biological warfare research station, where horrific animal experimentation goes on. . . .

Both Cliff Goodman and Ronnie Lee only served a third of their sentence and were both paroled after 12 months in the spring of 1976.

Being in jail had affected both of the Bicester Two, but in totally different ways. Cliff Goodman came out of prison with just one thought: he didn't want to go back inside. He decided he wasn't a revolutionary and wanted to stick to strictly legal campaigning in the future. Sadly, whilst in prison, Cliff decided to turn informer and gave the police a great deal of information about the use of radios by the Band of Mercy. For this act of treachery, Cliff was given the title of the movement's first 'grass' (police informer).

The Birth of the Animal Liberation Front

Ronnie, on the other hand, was given a new sense of determination and realized there was widespread public support for animal liberation illegal direct action. Whilst in prison Ronnie read widely on the subject of the labor movement.

With this knowledge and his pure determination, he started to plan a more revolutionary animal liberation group, a group that could indeed achieve animal liberation. . . .

Upon his release Ronnie gathered together the remains of the Band of Mercy. He was also able to find a couple dozen more new recruits for the illegal direct action animal liberation movement. Under Ronnie's gaze the new gathering (of approximately 30 people) was able to plan its future. With Ronnie as a leading light, the group could develop and expand the work of the Band of Mercy. This was a revolutionary group and everyone knew it.

The only problem for the group was the name the Band of Mercy. The name was no longer appropriate. It didn't fit the new revolutionary feel. A new name was needed. A name that would haunt the animal abusers. A name whose very mention could symbolize a whole ideology of a revolutionary movement. A name that was more than a name. With all this in mind Ronnie selected the name the Animal Liberation Front; the A.L.F.

> *"Latent violence is behind every law, every rule, and every requirement in any collectivist undertaking."*

Socialists Encourage Violent Extremism

Brian Paterson

Socialism, Brian Paterson argues in the following viewpoint, is a political system based on violence and coercion. According to Paterson, socialism creates no new wealth or property but rather redistributes what already exists. He insists that the forced redistribution of wealth inherent in socialism makes it a poor choice for the twenty-first century. Brian Paterson is a mainframe and PC computer programmer who originated and maintains the www.screwedupworld.com Web site.

As you read, consider the following questions:
1. In the author's opinion, why do some people consider capitalism a universal monster?
2. According to Paterson, in a socialist society, what will happen if you ignore a command to redistribute your wealth?
3. What new political ideas did the Enlightenment offer the Western public forum, in Paterson's opinion?

Although in many ways I do not fit the sensitive, New-Age guy profile, I do enjoy reading some authors of a transformational or modern philosophical bent. And over the years, I've noticed that many New-Age type people whom I either read about or talk with seem to accept some form of collectivism as a given in progressive thinking.

This was brought home to me while reading an article in *Yoga Journal* by someone who was emphasizing to readers that their life challenges were their own and not the cause of some external force. In making his point, he put forth a list of things to which people commonly attribute their unhappiness (spouse, job, boss, etc.) and concluded that list with, "no, not even Capitalism is to blame". And it wasn't intended sarcastically.

The columnist's easy use of Capitalism as a universal monster struck me as rather odd. I do know that references to the goodness of collectivism are common in New-Age or "progressive" writings and I would be the first to agree that having less attachment to material things and sharing freely with others is undoubtedly a more evolved outlook.

Nothing New Is Created

But collectivism—Socialism—does neither. First of all, it stresses enormous attachment to (usually others') possessions and emanates from the very un-New-Age outlook of "scarcity" thinking. Socialism rarely creates anything new; rather it looks at what free people have already created and redistributes it, according to what is popular at the time.

Secondly, it is a system based entirely on coercion and violence—forcing other people at gunpoint to do things with their possessions and their livelihoods that they would not have done by choice. Over-the-top hyperbole, you say? Try ignoring a command to redistribute your wealth. If you do so long enough, people will eventually come to your house with guns, take you away and incarcerate you. We call it going to prison for tax evasion.

That latent violence is behind every law, every rule, and every requirement in any collectivist undertaking. And it has been my experience that, just as Mom always said, any matter brought to bear through violence or the threat thereof, is only a short-term solution at best. No matter how noble the cause—whether you are planning to cure cancer or distribute food—taking people's money at gunpoint is not a morally sound long-term proposition. And, no, the fact that you get to vote on it doesn't make it any more so.

Socialism Creates Terror

The left's vision was man as a selfless slave of the state, and the state as the omniscient manager of the economy. However, instead of prosperity, happiness and freedom, Communism and Socialism produced nothing but poverty, misery and terror (witness Soviet Russia, North Korea and Cuba, among others). Their system had to fail, because it was based on a lie. You cannot create freedom and happiness by destroying individual rights; and you cannot create prosperity by negating the mind and evading the laws of economics.

Edwin A. Locke, *Capitalism Magazine*, May 1, 2002.

If I were to suggest that you should be forced to work unpaid for two days each week but you get to vote on where, you would be outraged. You would correctly call it slavery. Yet when I propose that you can work wherever you like, but I will take the fruits of two (or three) days from each week's labor, you wouldn't bat an eye. You would correctly call it taxation. Then, when that money is handed out to a properly anointed cause, those doing the handing can proclaim what a generous people we are, never addressing the awkward fact that the money was in fact "contributed" more out of the wish to avoid federal prison rather than anything resembling authentic generosity.

Individuals Choose What Works

If people voluntarily choose to live and share in a communal situation, I think that's great. I personally would become highly annoyed living in close quarters with a group and having to vote on everything that happens. But, thanks to the wisdom of our forefathers when they created a Constitutional Republic, you don't have to live my way either.

As opposed to in a simple majority-rule democracy, you can choose what works for you with the comforting knowledge that it cannot ever be voted on by people you don't even know. And that actually sounds pretty progressive to me. For although we may take it as self evident today, it was at that time truly new thought born of the Enlightenment movement in Europe. The importance of that can't be over-emphasized—that rather than a new spin on old ideas, it was thought that had never before happened in the Western public forum.

So, modern pundits notwithstanding maybe the "new" ideas of the 1970's are actually more rooted in weary Marxism of the 1870's than in the authentically new age thinking of the 1770's.

"Without a mass Marxist party offering clear socialist alternatives to capitalism people will turn to all sorts of strange actions and ideas for answers."

Socialism Would Benefit Society

John Fisher

The reconstruction of society along socialist lines will end the anger and cynicism of youth caused by the violence and destructiveness of capitalism, John Fisher claims in the following viewpoint. Fisher argues that young people who reject American culture by embracing radical religious views are seeking an alternative to the decaying values of capitalism that only socialism can provide. Further, he maintains that the benefits of socialism offer young people a future that capitalism cannot match. John Fisher is an executive member of the Socialist Alliance, a socialist organization in England.

As you read, consider the following questions:
1. In Fisher's opinion, why are Marxists not surprised by the actions of John Walker and Charles Bishop?
2. According to the author, why were Walker and Bishop attracted to religious fanaticism?
3. Who will guide the forward movement of humanity as a whole, in Fisher's opinion?

John Fisher, "Domestic Symptoms of Capitalism in Decay," *Youth for International Socialism*, www.newyouth.com, January 7, 2002. Copyright © 2002 by Wellred. Reproduced by permission.

Recently an American by the name of John Walker was found in the ranks of the [Muslim fundamentalist] Taliban. A young boy, Charles Bishop, also recently flew a small plane into a tall Florida office building. In his pocket was found a hand written note expressing support for [Arab terrorist Osama] bin Laden. To many these occurrences are shocking, to Marxists they are no surprise. Global capitalism is in the epoch of its senile decay. Not even suburban America is safe from the cancer of this rotten system.

Unknowingly the two mentioned individuals have expressed discontent not just with American culture, but with capitalism as a whole. They have rejected American society, but have embraced reactionary religious fanaticism. Without a clear alternative to the problems and filth capitalism has created they have turned into the shock troops of reaction. Without a mass Marxist party offering clear socialist alternatives to capitalism people will turn to all sorts of strange actions and ideas for answers.

Angry Youth

Why though is the rottenness of capitalism popping up so close to home? Today's suburban kids have "everything they need, they go to school, they have their TVs, their video games, their music."

Young Americans and Western Europeans are angry. But again, why? The apologists of capital say, "what is wrong with these kids, they have everything they want!" They're angry because the system of capitalism offers them no real future. On the news they see wars raging in ex-colonial nations thanks to the consequences of imperialism. In their own country they see mass violence, such as school shootings (yet another product of the American culture created by a decaying capitalism). In their own homes they see their parents at each other's throats over money, it is no wonder violence and anger is all the "rage" in the West among the youth. Multiply this scenario by millions with thousands of different variations and it is no surprise the cancer of capitalism is popping up in the intestines of the beast itself.

How does this end? How does the anger and cynicism of the youth end? It will end along with the rotten system which created it—capitalism. The answer is not the injection of hypocritical religious morals into the schools but the conscious revolutionary reconstruction of society along socialist lines.

Socialism Offers a New Social and Economic Order

The Socialist Party strives to establish a radical democracy that places people's lives under their own control—a non-racist, classless, feminist, socialist society in which people cooperate at work, at home, and in the community.

Socialism is not mere government ownership, a welfare state, or a repressive bureaucracy. Socialism is a new social and economic order in which workers and consumers control production and community residents control their neighborhoods, homes, and schools. The production of society is used for the benefit of all humanity, not for the private profit of a few. Socialism produces a constantly renewed future by not plundering the resources of the earth.

Michigan Socialist Party, www.michigansocialist.net, 2004.

How will this happen though? Not through religious fundamentalism, not through any sort of reforms even. It will end through the building of a mass party of the proletariat. Only through the conscious efforts of the working class guided by an aware Marxist leadership will the socialist reconstruction of society be possible and with that the movement forward of humanity as a whole.

"The FBI now considers . . .'ecoterrorism'
. . . to be America's most serious form of
domestic terror."

Radical Environmentalists Are Terrorists

Brad Knickerbocker

Brad Knickerbocker argues in the following viewpoint that attacks by radical environmentalists such as the Earth Liberation Front (ELF) are now considered serious acts of terrorism. While ELF's acts of vandalism and arson have not yet physically hurt anyone, Knickerbocker contends that the group has threatened to use guns if necessary to achieve its ends. Moreover, the U.S. government defines terrorism as the "unlawful use of force and violence against persons or property," which clearly includes ELF acts such as burning down construction projects and blowing up SUVs. Brad Knickerbocker is a staff writer for the *Christian Science Monitor.*

As you read, consider the following questions:
1. According to Knickerbocker, until the San Diego fire, what was ELF's largest attack?
2. Why is it difficult to arrest or prosecute ELF ecoterrorists, in the author's opinion?
3. In Knickerbocker's opinion, how do mainstream environmentalists regard ELF's tactics?

Brad Knickerbocker, "Firebrands of 'Ecoterrorism' Set Sights on Urban Sprawl," *The Christian Science Monitor*, August 6, 2003. Copyright © 2003 by The Christian Science Publishing Society. All rights reserved. Reproduced by permission.

Environmental activism's darker side is turning from wild nature to the urban jungle. Among its targets: posh housing developments, car dealerships hawking sport utility vehicles, and military-recruiting stations.

The latest attack came [in early August 2003] when a large condominium project under construction in an upscale San Diego neighborhood burned to the ground. A banner stretched across the charred site read: "If you build it—we will burn it. The E.L.F.s are mad." In e-mails to regional newspapers, the Earth Liberation Front (ELF) claimed responsibility for the conflagration that also damaged nearby homes.

Domestic Terrorism

Property damage in the name of environmental protection dates back to the "monkey wrenching" advocated by groups like Earth First. But trashing logging trucks and driving spikes into old-growth trees pales in comparison to recent events—arson and vandalism of luxury homes, and violent assaults on the symbols of urban sprawl. SUVs have been vandalized or firebombed in Santa Cruz, Calif., Eugene, Ore., and Erie, Pa. At the US Navy recruiting headquarters in Montgomery, Ala., cars were spray painted with antiwar messages and a truck was set on fire. The FBI now considers such attacks—dubbed "ecoterrorism"—to be America's most serious form of domestic terror.

Still, it's not clear why activists targeted the San Diego apartments. Despite the size of the complex—at 1,500 units, it's one of southern California's largest apartment-construction projects—the La Jolla Crossroads was hardly controversial, raising nary an eyebrow when plans came before city officials a few years back.

"It wasn't a big item on our radar," says Richard Miller, chair of the local Sierra Club chapter. The condos did take up open space and will of course contribute to urban growth and traffic, Mr. Miller says. But on the other hand, the project met environmentalists' goals, providing housing for hundreds of people in a fairly small space and setting aside apartments for poor and middle-income residents.

Until the San Diego fire, the largest such attack was the 1998 burning of a new ski resort in Vail, Colo., which critics

Earth Liberation Actions in 2002

The total direct actions for Earth liberation that occurred in 2002 were 53, down from 65 in 2001, an 18% decrease. January was by far the busiest month with 10 actions recorded.

There were 49 actions in the US, in 16 different states, and 4 in Canada, in 2 provinces. Oregon was the most active state with 10 actions recorded, followed by Virginia with 7. California had 6 and Pennsylvania recorded 5. . . .

New developments dominated the issues focused on with 13 actions taken against various new homes and building projects. Forest issues accounted for 10 actions while cars and SUVs took 8. 91 vehicles were targeted.

Monthly Totals		States/Provinces	
January	10	AZ	01
February	02	CA	06
March	02	CO	02
April	05	IN	01
May	02	KY	01
June	05	MA	02
July	06	ME	01
August	04	MI	01
September	06	MN	04
October	06	MT	01
November	01	OR	10
December	04	PA	05
		TX	01
		UT	02
		VA	07
		WA	04
		BC	03
		ONT	01

Issues

development	13
forest/environment related	10
cars & SUVs	08
GMO	06
police & government	06
powerlines	05
corporate	01
education	01
golf	01
olympics	01
sexism	01

North American Animal Liberation Front press office, 2002.

had said would eliminate a vast habitat for the threatened Canada lynx.

The fundamental factor behind the ELF—apparently the main motivator of such attacks—is that "the profit motive caused and reinforced by the capitalist society is destroying all life on this planet," according to the ELF website. "The only way, at this point in time, to stop that continued destruction of life is to . . . take the profit motive out of killing."

Violence Is Allowed

ELF "guidelines" include taking "all necessary precautions against harming any animal, human and non-human." But they also include a call to "inflict economic damage on those profiting from the destruction and exploitation of the natural environment."

An ELF "communiqué" taking responsibility for last September's [2002] firebombing of a US Forest Service research station in Pennsylvania declared: "While innocent life will never be harmed in any action we undertake, where it is necessary, we will no longer hesitate to pick up the gun to implement justice, and provide the needed protection for our planet that decades of legal battles, pleading, protest, and economic sabotage have failed . . . to achieve."

The group's website includes a 37-page how-to manual titled "Setting Fires With Electrical Timers."

The ELF is an ideological cousin to the Animal Liberation Front (ALF), a group that began in England about 12 years ago as a more radical alternative to Earth First. The ELF claimed its first "action" in the United States in 1997—releasing wild horses and torching a US Bureau of Land Management corral near Burns, Ore.

Since then, it's claimed credit for what it says are hundreds of attacks and some $50 million in damages. The FBI does not dispute those figures.

Few Arrests

Few arrests or prosecutions have followed from the violent actions of environmentalists or animal-rights advocates—and, indeed, most such crimes remain unsolved. One "eco-terrorist" on the FBI's "wanted" list is Michael James Scarpitti, accused of torching concrete mixing trucks and Oregon logging equipment.

The ELF has no central location, leadership, or hierarchy. It's organized into autonomous cells that work independently and anonymously. Its "communiqués" and website are managed by supporters without clear links to ELF crimes.

While mainstream environmentalists generally reject ELF tactics, some activists object to the portrayal of the group's assaults on property as "terrorism": So far, at least, the vandalism, even the violence, has not caused any death or major injury.

But the federal government defines "terrorism" as "the unlawful use of force and violence against persons or property to intimidate or coerce a government, the civilian population, or any segment thereof, in furtherance of political or social objectives"—a definition that would appear to match the aims and activities of the ELF.

"Acts of [environmental sabotage] are entirely justified and are, indeed, both necessary and effective."

Ecoterrorism Is Justified

Emily Kumpel

Radical environmentalism is justified because less violent tactics have not proven effective in stopping the destruction of the environment, Emily Kumpel argues in the following viewpoint. She insists that many radical environmentalists address the immediate need to protect what is left of the environment at any cost. Although Kumpel is uncomfortable with the destructiveness of ecoterrorist acts, she supports them because they effect necessary change. Emily Kumpel is a student at Johns Hopkins University.

As you read, consider the following questions:
1. What is deep ecology, in the author's opinion?
2. What is the central goal behind ecoterror, according to the author?
3. Why have strategies to crack down on ecoterrorism not worked, according to Kumpel?

The immediate danger facing the environment and the human cause of this destruction are clear to many activists around the globe. Also acknowledged is that something must be done. However, there are many different types of environmentalists out there with a wide range of tactics and philosophies used to justify their actions and guide them in their defense of the wild. One movement of extreme environmental activism has been dubbed "ecoterrorism" or "ecotage". Ecoterrorism is defined in the dictionary as "terrorism or sabotage committed in the name of environmental causes," while these groups themselves describe it as nonviolent direct action. According to the FBI, ecoterrorism is "the use or threatened use of violence of a criminal nature against innocent victims or property by an environmentally-oriented, subnational group for environmental-political reasons, or aimed at an audience beyond the target, often of a symbolic nature." David Foreman, the founder of a self-described "radical" environmental group Earth First!, asserts that, "We can have big wilderness, and we can reintroduce extirpated species, but unless the fact that there are way too many people on the earth is dealt with, unless the idea that the world is a resource for us to use is dealt with, unless humans can find their way home again, then the problems will continue."

Many ecoterrorists ascribe to what is known as deep ecology, and their actions address the immediate need to protect what is left—preventing, for example, the logging of a particular forest or the death of a single whale—as well as suggesting a change in the fundamental way we think of ourselves and of our place in nature. As Foreman explained, ". . . we had to offer a fundamental challenge to Western civilization." The group's motto is "No compromise in defense of Mother Earth."

Earth First! uses "confrontation, guerrilla theater, direct action and civil disobedience to fight for wild places and life processes." While they do not actually "condone or condemn monkey wrenching, ecotage, or other forms of property destruction," they do provide a network for activists to discuss creative ways of opposing environmental destruction. According to Bill McKibben, "Earth First! and the few other groups like it have a purpose, and that purpose is defense of the wild, the natural, the nonhuman." However, there is a line between civil disobedience and nonviolent direct action in that the latter includes monkey wrenching and criminal destruction of property. Other groups, such as the Earth Liberation Front (ELF), which broke off from Earth First! when others wanted to "mainstream" the group, and the Animal Liberation Front (ALF) are well known for their acts of ecotage. According to the FBI, the ELF and the ALF are "serious terrorist threats(s)." Tactics include disabling logging machinery, placing activists in front of whaling ships, destroying airstrips, spiking trees, and arson.

Deep Ecology Is a Defense

How do these environmentalists justify destroying human creations for the sake of a single living thing or small forest? This movement finds its defense in deep ecology and ecocentric ethics, major religions and new age philosophy, and, sometimes, conventional wisdom.

In defense of ecoterrorism, I will put forward that these actions are dictated by the Earth Liberation Front Guidelines, which are as follows: "1. To inflict economic damage on those profiting from the destruction and exploitation of the natural environment. 2. To reveal and educate the public on the atrocities committed against the earth and all species that populate it. 3. To take all necessary precautions against harming any animal, human and non-human."

The central goal behind ecoterror beliefs is to shift the focus away from humans and onto the entire ecosystem. McKibben describes Earth First! as "one of the purest examples of putting the rest of creation ahead of exclusively human needs." Changing the anthropocentric view of the environment is the heart of many environmental philosophies. However, these philosophies often dictate only how we think, not our actions. Ecoterrorists take this to heart and use traditionally drastic measures to accomplish their goals.

First, we as humans are not superior and therefore either all living things should be treated the same, or the whole of the community should come before the good of the individual. The first is a biotic view of ecology, incorporating Albert

Schweitzer's notion of a "reverence for life." In resolving conflicts between man and nature, he suggests this order: 1. self-defense 2. proportionality 3. minimum wrong 4. distributive justice 5. restitutive justice. Ecoterrorists protect the life of both living beings and natural systems from human destruction when the human destruction is a function of our wants, not our needs. In Colorado, for example, ecoterrorists committed an incredibly costly act of ecotage, burning five buildings at the Vail Ski Resort in 1998. The ski resort was constructed despite the outcries of the public and environmentalists, as the company clear-cut what was supposed to remain untouched wilderness. While human property was destroyed, no humans or other living things were harmed. "They ask, why is more ski terrain, miles of roads, bathrooms and a warming house more important than the habitat of creatures man has already pushed to the brink of extinction?" This protection by ecotage—while extreme by many standards—is justified by Schweitzer's system. Humans had no claim to self-defense, the proportional gain for our species was not enough, there was no way to do a minimum wrong, and there is so little land left that there is no fair way to make up the destruction in another area. And, if we accept that all life should be respected and cared for, then we should do all we can to protect life from human destruction.

Earth Liberation Front Guidelines

1. To cause as much economic damage as possible to a given entity that is profiting off the destruction of the natural environment and life for selfish greed and profit,

2. To educate the public on the atrocities committed against the environment and life,

3. To take all necessary precautions against harming life.

North American Earth Liberation Front press office, 2001.

In one of the most well known defenses of environmentalism, Aldo Leopold upholds that, "A thing is right when it tends to preserve the integrity, stability, and beauty of the biotic community. It is wrong when it tends otherwise." We have an obligation to uphold the stability of the system. Ecoterrorism serves to protect the biotic community using methods that, while destroying human creations, still do not benefit the community. Human creations are not included as a part of this biotic community, and most methods of ecotage in the environmental movement serve to protect wild areas from human expansion. Any infringement by humans into this area would disrupt our ecosystem's integrity, stability, and beauty; therefore, it is wrong. Ecoterrorist acts are consequently right because they protect those values.

The Land Ethic View

The land ethic view of environmental philosophy incorporates both living and nonliving entities, and it puts the stability of the community above individual lives. In this belief, humans have no superiority in nature, and we, as humans, are responsible for righting our wrongs—for example, reintroducing species to an area if we caused their extinction. The strongest criticism of this approach is also the strongest support for ecotage; it "condones sacrificing the good of individuals to the good of the whole," which is indeed just what the movement is doing. Bill McKibben also suggests that "individual suffering—animal or human—might be less important that the suffering of species, ecosystems, the planet."

The FBI considers these ecoterrorist organizations to be domestic terrorist groups, and many mainstream environmentalists working to protect the same wilderness areas are opposed to monkey wrenching. Environmentalists, politicians, business leaders, and the public alike have all brought up many arguments against the use of ecotage. Some argue that we as humans are a part of nature and our evolution has led us to superiority over the rest of the environment. Therefore we should be in control of the environment, letting our own natural evolution take its course. By downsizing our lives to preserve the environment we are going against the natural course of things.

Ecoterrorists (and others) reply that we are addicted to consumerism as well as growth and expansion. Just because that is the way it has always been does not mean that it is right; evolution changes things. Perhaps our evolution is not in taking control of the earth, but in learning to stop our growing and settle down. [David] Orr states that economic growth is the target of our society because growth is "the normal state of things." However, our natural resources are finite, and can only hold so many people and offer so much, therefore, economic growth has to be finite at some point as well. People, especially workers, do things because that's just the way it is and how it's always been "And we don't want to change," McKibben suggests. "Jim wants to log as he always has. I want to be able to drive as I always have and go on living in the large house I live in and so on." As a result we have begun to decline as human beings by staying the same, because material goods are no longer fulfilling and there is no more meaningful work left to be done. The cultural sickness dubbed "affluenza" is used to describe our addiction to material goods and the absurdity of it all. Ecotage contributes to reducing our lifestyles and the material goods and lifestyles within. . . .

Extreme Action Is Not Pragmatic

Others, especially more traditional environmentalists, argue that extreme action is simply not pragmatic in the society in which we live. According to this argument, ecoterrorism ignores the culture and the political system we work in, and we cannot just disregard that. They argue that ecoterrorists make it hard for other environmental activists working from within the system because they lose respect for all other environmental causes. In our current political system, there are so many things that are going on in voter's minds and environmentalism is only one of many. Equating environmentalism with extremism is not going to help gain any votes.

However, according to an ABC reporter who investigated the ecotage movement, ecoterrorists have exhausted all of the traditional options before turning to destruction. ". . . though there are many many environmental groups out there who use traditional approaches like lobbying Congress and protesting timber sales, ELF regards mainstream groups as sell-outs, and corporate puppets . . . they saw these techniques fail time and time again to stop the march of industry on nature." The Earth First! website asks readers if they are tired of, "namby-pamby environmental groups" and "overpaid corporate environmentalists who suck up to bureaucrats and industry." Ecoterrorists are not looking to uphold the system and work within it, but are instead looking to change people's attitudes and see extreme actions as the only way to both protect the immediate needs of the environment and drastically inspire a change of attitude. These acts probably do make environmentalists as a whole lose credibility in the political and economic world, though ecoterrorists argue that the political, economic, and moral world we currently live in is what itself needs to be changed and working within the system will not accomplish that.

Ecoterrorism does challenge the way we think about the system and many activists' view of how to work within the system. Yet their methods have proven effective in saving individual wild lands and living beings.

Another argument against ecoterrorism is that even though many activists say that they aren't harming human lives, destruction of property is destroying people's jobs and is therefore destroying livelihoods. A contributor to *Nature* magazine described Earth First!'s methods as showing a "deep insensitivity to human suffering." One of the newer arguments against ecotage in the United States [after the September 11, 2001, terrorist attacks] is that if foreign terrorism is not acceptable, then domestic terrorism like ecotage is not acceptable either. Some environmentalists are even accused of "environmental fascism."

Environmental Destruction

But many also recognize that the environmental destruction that humans are creating because of our view of the earth as a resource for our own use is threatening our health and that of our children. Richard Falk calls for tougher strategies in order to produce results, suggesting that we, "engage concrete sources of resistance, including human depravity and greed . . . moral concern is serious only if it includes active participation in ongoing struggles against injustice and suffering." McKibben says of deep ecology's reductionist approach, ". . . they are extreme solutions, but we live in an extreme time. . . . If industrial civilization is ending nature, it is not utter silliness to talk about ending—or, at least, transforming—industrial civilization," and that "the thinking is more radical than

111

the action." Many actions we collectively take, such as the nuclear arms buildup and our cultural obsession with fast food and Coca-Cola, are all considered irrational, yet we do it. So why not ecoterrorism? Links have been made between slavery and today's exploitation of natural resources such as fossil fuels and animals. Radical actions ended slavery, and radicalism powered the civil rights movement, native independence, and many other great progressive moves throughout history. So why not ecoterrorism? Nature is dying, according to McKibben, and he urges us to give the end of nature our best fight. "We are different from the rest of the natural order, for the single reason that we possess the possibility of self-restraint, or choosing some other way."

And the suggestions to crackdown on ecoterrorism post 9-11 have not worked. Richard Berman, the executive director of the Center for Consumer Freedom, asked Congress to cut funding to ecoterrorist groups, much like it did to the Al Qaeda network [responsible for the September 11 attacks]. He asked that their nonprofit status be taken away, or that groups like People for the Ethical Treatment of Animals and Physicians Committee for Responsible Medicine that have supposedly given support to ecoterrorist groups in the past be reprimanded in some way. However, this proposal did not gain much support. So far, the ELF and ALF members have been very effective in avoiding the authorities because they are so decentralized and act within cells of one to several members. Funding does not seem to be a key issue for the group.

While ecoterrorists describe themselves as subscribers to deep ecology, I find that the strongest arguments to justify their actions instead come from a mixture of many environmental philosophies. Indeed, based on any view of the environment that puts the emphasis away from humans, I find it hard not to support the use of ecoterrorism to prevent destruction.

Ecoterrorism Is Justified

Yet I also feel myself so entrenched in this system of the way it has always been that I find it hard to advocate acts of sabotage against the political and economic structure of our world.

I think that acts of ecotage are entirely justified and are, indeed, both necessary and effective, yet I cannot imagine myself being able to actually commit ecoterrorism. Looking at radical animal rights groups like People for the Ethical Treatment of Animals, I entirely disagree with most of their tactics, and yet, it was their tactics that caused me to become vegan. Like many supporters of "extreme" environmental activists, I may disagree with the destructive and damaging nature of such tactics, yet I cannot argue with their effectiveness.

Periodical Bibliography

The following articles have been selected to supplement the diverse views presented in this chapter.

Diane Alden	"Destroyer of Worlds," NewsMax.com, August 18, 2001.
Alex Callinicos	"The Case for Revolutionary Socialism," *Z Magazine*, December 7, 2003.
Brian Carnell	"Extent of Animal Rights Extremism in the United States," AnimalRights.net, May 14, 2000.
Dan Gabriel	"Extremist Groups Target Businesses and People," *Insight on the News*, May 28, 2001.
William T. Johnson	"The Bible on Environmental Conservation: A 21st Century Prescription," *Electronic Green Journal*, 2000.
Patrik Jonsson	"Tracing an Animal-Rights Philosophy," *Christian Science Monitor*, October 9, 2001.
Roger Kimball	"The Death of Socialism," *New Criterion*, April 2002.
Edwin A. Locke	"Anti-Globalization: The Left's Violent Assault on Global Prosperity," *Capitalism Magazine*, May 1, 2002.
Adrian R. Morrison	"Personal Reflections on the Animal-Rights Phenomenon," *Perspectives in Biology and Medicine*, Winter 2001.
Jim Motavalli	"A Movement to Grant Legal Protections to Animals Is Gathering Force," Environmental News Network, May 2, 2003. www.enn.com.
Ralph Nader	"Corporate Socialism," *Washington Post*, July 18, 2002.
William P. Orth	"U.S. Workers Face a No-Win Situation: Less Hours, Less Pay, More Work," *Socialist*, October 2003.
Dennis Prager	"Socialism Kills," TownHall.com, September 2, 2003.
Southern Poverty Law Center	"From Push to Shove," *Intelligence Report*, 2003.
Workers World	"Which Road to Socialism?" December 25, 2003. www.workers.org.

Chapter Preface

White supremacist organizations such as the Ku Klux Klan, the National Alliance, and the Creativity Movement (formerly the World Church of the Creator) have been male dominated since their founding. Women involved in these organizations have traditionally played supportive, usually subservient roles to men in the group. The division of roles along gender lines was clear: men were active in the group while women stayed home and bore and raised children. Indeed, women were usually recruited to these groups for the purpose of carrying the next generation of the white race. For many white supremacist women, this homebound, reproductive role was enough. However, late in the twentieth century women began to take more active, often violent roles in supremacist groups. Women for Aryan Unity, a women's white supremacist organization, now encourages women "to stand by their men and take up their weapons and battle cry if the men should fall." Women's roles in supremacist organizations have evolved to include the active promotion of hate and violence. Kirsten Kaiser, married for nine years to a member of the neo-Nazi National Alliance says, "It seems to me that the true believers, the women, are even more violent than the men."

Kathleen M. Blee, author of *Inside Organized Racism: Women in the Hate Movement*, maintains that while some women have drifted into racist organizations—usually because of their involvement with a man who has ties to the group—many women have sought out white supremacy organizations on their own. She contends that they are just as resolute in their commitment to racism as men in such groups and just as ready to turn to violence. Blee argues that "in a number of groups women are not only cheerleaders, but are active participants and planners." Further, her research has shown that racist groups that attract younger people—skinheads and neo-Nazis, for example—are more likely to attract women who want an active role. Blee insists, "These young women expect to be part of the violence of these groups."

Mark Potok of the Southern Poverty Law Center, an organization that tracks U.S. extremist group activity, concurs with Blee. His research shows that racist groups are actively recruiting young women who are not afraid of violence. He explains, "There is so much talk within the movement about the difficulty of finding good Aryan female warriors, that now it is being acted upon." Lisa Tuner, founder of the Women's Frontier, an offshoot of the neo-Nazi World Church of the Creator, notes, "Everyone is starting to realize that if we are going to overcome in this struggle, we are going to have to do it together—man and woman—side by side."

Women in white supremacist organizations have proven that they can be just as steadfast in the promotion of the racist cause as their male counterparts. In the following chapter authors debate whether white supremacist groups promote hate and violence.

> *"The 'race war' advocates are now reaching high schools, colleges and official military units through the Internet."*

White Supremacist Groups Promote Hate and Violence

Carl Rowan

Carl Rowan was a syndicated columnist and authored *The Coming Race War in America.* In the following viewpoint taken from a 1999 column, he argues that the dire predictions he made in his 1996 book about the dangers posed by white supremacists are coming true. According to Rowan, white supremacists now promote hate and violence against minorities more and more efficiently using the Internet. Moreover, he maintains, these hate-mongers are amassing illegal arms with which to conduct a race war in America.

As you read, consider the following questions:

1. How did Richard Butler respond after Buford O. Furrow shot five people at a Jewish community center in 1999, as related by the author?
2. What "one-man forays" does Rowan describe?
3. Why does Rowan think his "alarmist" book is even more pertinent today?

Carl Rowan, "The Creeping Race War," *Liberal Opinion Week*, vol. 10, August 30, 1999, p. 10. Copyright © 1999 by North American Syndicate. Reproduced by permission.

[I]n 1999] after Buford O. Furrow shot five people at a Jewish community center in Los Angeles and gunned down postal worker Joseph Ileto because "he was nonwhite and worked for the federal government," the white supremacist leader of the Idaho-based Aryan Nations said of Furrow: "He was a good soldier."

"I cannot condemn what he did. He was very respected among us," added Richard Butler, leader of a group that is notorious for advocating violence as a means of making the United States an all-white nation.

Not an Aberration

Butler's words suggest that Furrow was not just a deranged loner when he launched his attack on Jews and nonwhites. Just as Benjamin Nathaniel Smith was more than a loner when he staged a shooting attack on Jews, blacks and Asians in Illinois and Indiana over the [1999] Fourth of July weekend. Just as Timothy J. McVeigh and Terry L. Nichols were not just "lone wolf" nuts when they perpetrated the 1995 bombing of the Alfred P. Murrah federal building in Oklahoma City, killing 168 people.

The bigots within America who hate blacks, Jews, "foreigners," immigrants, Muslims and the federal government are carrying out an unholy war, but it is a war of snipers, isolated shootings and bombings, and one-man forays so far. It may soon become more organized—and worse.

So it is wise that Columbine High School in Colorado reopens this week [in August 1999] under conditions of heightened security. It is prudent that schools across America have taken steps to prevent outbursts of violence by those caught in the dark clutches of the haters. It would be well for the rest of us to be on guard.

A Race War

In 1996, I published a book warning that this society was imperiled by white racists who threatened to kill Jews, deport or kill blacks, wage war on unfavorable judges and federal facilities, and eventually provoke a tragic race war. I made the mistake of titling that book *The Coming Race War in America*, thus scaring the hell out of many reviewers and people who

Anti-Semitic Incidents Year-by-Year National Totals 1980–1999

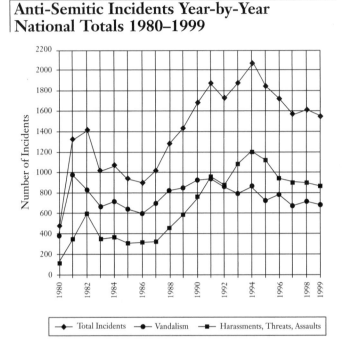

The number of anti-Semitic incidents documented by the Anti-Defamation League (ADL) fell to a total of 1,547 incidents from 1,611 in 1998, a 4 percent decrease. Of the instances of anti-Semitism in 1999, there were 868 cases of harassment (down 3 percent from 896 in 1998), and 679 acts of vandalism (down 5 percent from 715 in 1998). Harassment and vandalism incidents represent 56 percent and 44 percent of the total incidents, respectively, which represents the same proportion as in 1998. ADL's 1998 *Audit* reported 896 incidents of harassment (56 percent of the total) and 715 (44 percent) instances of anti-Semitic vandalism.

Anti-Defamation League, "1999 Audit of Anti-Semitic Incidents," 1999.

branded it "alarmist" without reading it. I cited the 800 or so "militias" and the assorted venomous groups in America that had made as their "bible" a book by William Pierce called *The Turner Diaries*, in which the script for the Oklahoma City bombing was set forth in chilling detail. That book also set forth a plan for the extermination of blacks, Jews and unwanted immigrants.

My "alarmist" book is more pertinent, its documentation

more chilling, today than it was in 1996, because the haters have their war more on track. I am more alarmed now that I have seen Tom Metzger, leader of California's White Aryan Resistance (WAR), declare, "Good hunting, lone wolves" as he calls for a second civil war in exhorting his soldiers to act "in any way you see fit" against immigrants. The "crazy" single killers all have commanders giving orders.

Since 1995, the FBI and other law enforcement agencies have moved against the Viper Militia and other paramilitary groups that were amassing illegal arms and clearly constituted a threat of violence. That provoked a movement away from group actions. To foil FBI and police infiltrators, as I predicted in my book, the move has been to "lone wolf" and "good soldier" violence, with Internet and telephone messages and books by Pierce and other racists setting forth the battle cries and the targets.

The "race war" advocates are now reaching high schools, colleges and official military units through the Internet in ways they never could through books and pamphlets. Thus they have exposed us all to the threat of sudden death.

The problem America faces is far beyond the need to get psychiatrists to a small number of "sick" souls. It is not enough for schools, synagogues, black churches and non-white facilities to increase security. We must somehow get all of white America out of denial about the magnitude of "Christian Identity" racism and madness in this society.

The "disciples" and "soldiers" of Butler and Metzger will kill anyone—anyone—they think stands in the way of their Aryan America. Their race war is on. We can waste no time learning more about who they are and where they next plan to strike. And our law enforcement people must act accordingly.

> "*[Morris] Dees focuses on the Klan and other white supremacy groups who's bark is worse than its bite 'to raise more money for the [Southern Poverty Law] center.'*"

The Danger from White Supremacist Groups Is Exaggerated

Adrian H. Krieg

Adrian H. Krieg argues in the following viewpoint that the Southern Poverty Law Center (SPLC) and other watchdog groups exaggerate the danger posed by white supremacists in order to enrich themselves. He maintains that by inflating the membership numbers of the Klu Klux Klan and other white supremacist groups, the SPLC can raise large amounts of money from frightened whites, especially Jewish people. Krieg insists that most of the groups targeted by the SPLC pose no real danger and are being harassed because of their political beliefs. Adrian H. Krieg is a political writer and historian.

As you read, consider the following questions:

1. Why does Krieg maintain that hate pays?
2. Why does the SPLC consider white, Anglo-Saxon males to be the primary purveyors of hate, according to the author?
3. What group does Krieg claim is the largest contributor to the SPLC?

Would be "Do Gooders" seem pressed to contribute to organizations that inform us of their profound well-meaning actions to save society from the evil political right. This has become one of the most profitable business enterprises in the nation. Having taken note of this, it seems to me that people of particularly poor judgment are the most insistent that we support their causes. Assuredly we find these people as the most fanatical members of our society; their religion is one of hate, they hate everything that contradicts their politically left dogma. A substantial number of businesses have grown out of this, which can be said . . . now constitute an entire industry, in many cases of extorting funds from innocent bystanders for the sole purpose of self enrichment. The Simon Wiesenthal Center and the JDL [Jewish Defense League], along with the World Jewish Congress [WJC], come to mind. One of the most successful and most profitable of all of this lot is The Southern Poverty Law Center [SPLC] of Montgomery, Alabama. Two things strike me as ironic: the name and location.

We must first come to the realization that the name seems to indicate some method of fighting poverty and that this is nothing but a ruse. In their 1998 Form 990 IRS return we learn that on line 26 "other salaries and wages" all four columns combined total $6,970,322.00 for total payroll, and a whopping $1,465,130.00 in pension and other benefits. (Line 27 & 28) We learn on the same page that the aggregate expenses for 1998 were $41,550,243.00, no paltry sum that! . . .

We do learn that their extremely well paid executive staffs earns from $65,192.00 up to $272,047.00, with an additional $6,972.00 in direct benefits. I wonder seriously how anyone can justify the trappings of pretending to save the poor and wretched on a salary that is almost twelve times the national average income. In fact, if you are a management job seeker, at least one with limited moral and ethical education, you might find that working for a firm that compensates its average executive staff with $163,683.00 to be an excellent idea. After all, seven times the average national income seems like a good deal especially when you live in Alabama that is on the bottom of [the] national food chain in income.

Just exactly what is it the SPLC does? Well, this is a somewhat nebulous issue since they expend close to fifty percent of their income on advertising and the raising of additional funds, and a large chunk in payroll. When I said, "Hate Pays" I was not kidding; direct public support to SPLC in 1998 was over 27 million dollars.

Government Contracts

To make things worse we learn that revenues from government contracts amounted to $88,692.00, and in addition other income was interest on savings $163,789.00 and dividends from securities of $214,024.00. I don't exactly know how much money you need to have invested to earn $370,000.00 plus in just interest, but I am sure that it's more than one million. We learn from the offices of Senator Strom Thurmond that SPLC had a budget of $9.5 million for 1999.

Just exactly what they did for the government worth over eighty-eight thousand dollars does however interest me. One contract was the US Air Force AFSCO command Hurlburt Field FL by special order executed by Rochelle D. Wiegman Lt. Col. USAF dated July 03/96. It was to Joe Roy editor of *Klanwatch*, one of SPLC printed organs. Now I have reviewed the entire published SPLC['s] list of so-called "Hate Groups" includ[ed in] *Klanwatch*, and find the information contained therein at least in part fabrication. *Klanwatch* lists 138 Ku Klux Klan organizations under 36 various names. Not one address is listed. Not the name of one individual member. All the information provided consists of the name of a town and state, something that any grade school student could put together. Another contract also from the Air Force was again at Hurlburt Field this time with USAF-SOS Special Operations School. They give classes 8 times a year on average 4.5 days and had Mr. Joe Roy speak twice as a "recognized area expert on domestic right wing extremist groups." I for one would be more than just interested [in] what was contained in Mr. Roy's talk "Threat in the United States". Moreover, why the US Air Force is at all involved with what is constitutionally a domestic state police matter could be explained at the very same time. And while we're at it if the Air Force does not know what the "Threats in the United States" are they must be in the wrong business. I thought that this is exactly what the FBI is supposed to protect us from domestically, and the Air Force internationally. It is my understanding that there is a present lawsuit by Dr. Robert Clarkson against the U.S. Air Force for illegal use of SPLC documentation in brainwashing our troops. Three past employees of SPLC, Mr. Balske, Deborah Ellis and Denis Sweet, a past Alabama legislator, all say that [Morris] Dees focuses on the Klan and other white supremacy groups who's bark is worse than its bite "to raise more money for the center". Going after the Klan has brought in millions of dollars, from across the nation. The fact that total Klan membership nationally is below 5000—less than .0035% of the population—seems not to play any part in money raising or in contributing decisions.

This then brings us to the militias that are another *cause de celebrant* for SPLC. The fact that 95% of these militias are benign simply is not part of the equation. While government agencies (FBI, BATF [Bureau of Alcohol, Tobacco and Firearms]) need to create villains to sustain their bloated budgets, SPLC working, often hand in glove with them, requires hate groups to obtain ever more contributions. That the successes of both government agencies and the private sector hate mongers have been more than just successful goes without saying. How many so-called hate groups are partially or wholly financed by various government agencies is also a matter of some conjecture. Often in joint and apparently orchestrated effort they persue the very same outcome. . . .

Hate Crimes

Hate Crimes [are] the latest of a long line of corrosive ideas pushed by the SPLC as well as the political left. George Orwell was first to write on the topic, first in an essay and then in his book *1984* calling it news-speak, a process of through language influencing a pre-plan[n]ed outcome, and of controlling people. We have already instituted a national practice of PC (Political Correctness) that is in fact Cultural Marxism. (CM) Through these processes the left has demonized any historic fact that does not meet the outcome goals of the political left and their academic stooges. In this cause history is being rewritten, consider movies and books like

Roots, *Amistad* and *Pocahontas*, historically not just inaccurate but totally wrong.

They represent the plagiarizing of history for the purpose of social change. This is taking place in our entire society in every venue. Even our language is under attack. Gay, Assault Rifle, Cop Killer Bullet, Peacekeepers, Hippie, Hispanic, Homophobic, Choice, Saturday Night Special, all these words have been created by leftist foundations so that issues can be twisted to their side of the argument. But of greater interest is the fact that none of those words and phrases they have created make any sense, nor are they definable in a lexicographer vernacular.

SPLC can well be categorized as a Dees enterprise. Morris Dees is from Shorter, Alabama. He studied at the University of Alabama School of Commerce. Together with Millary Fuller he set up Fuller & Dees Hart Dixie Products, giving him the "good old boy" appearance. The name was then changed to Fuller & Dees Marketing Group. After his marriage to Maureen he sold his 89% interest in the company to the Los Angeles Mirror Corp. for $5,150,000.00. . . .

Much amazing and confounding information can be learned from the SPLC Internet site. Things I did not know until today when I reviewed the site. First of all it appears that White Anglo Saxon males are the primary purveyors of hate because in the entire list of claimed hate groups no female, Hispanic, Homosexual, or Oriental hate groups appear; now that in itself is amazing. Can there be any doubt that such exist? Of 457 "Hate Groups" listed, 21 are claimed to be "Black Separatist" but when you go through the list you find only The House of David, and Nation of Islam listed. In fact a careful review of the entire list [reveals] listed groups that were obviously placed on the list to inflate the numbers. I know of one on the list who has just entered a lawsuit against SPLC, and one that is definitely not a Hate Group, but rather a newspaper with a circulation of over 10,000 and many that are mere figments of SPLC's imagination.

Benign Organizations Are Listed

Since no addresses are given it is impossible to validate the list, addresses which were in my opinion left off for a very good reason. Furthermore there are numerous organizations listed with rather benign names and purpose; among these are over 15 organizations containing the word Christian. A large number of Baptist and other Churches, Publishers, as well as numerous patriotic and conservative organizations are listed. The NAACP [National Association for the Advancement of Colored People] is not listed but the NAAWP (National Association for the Advancement of White People) is. . . . It only applies to Anglo Saxon males. No one else need apply!

All this in my opinion is for no other reason than to garnish funds from people stupid enough to contribute to SPLC.

Racist Groups Pose Little Danger

They collect millions of dollars for their crusades against hate groups, but do so-called "watchdog" organizations exaggerate the dangers posed by neo-Nazis and other racist movements? Laird Wilcox thinks so. A Kansas author and editor who has spent decades researching what he calls "fringe" groups, Mr. Wilcox says the total numbers of active, organized extremists on the right is not much more than 10,000.

"Because of their nature, it's very difficult to come up with firm numbers" for such groups, Mr. Wilcox says, but estimates "the militias are probably 5,000 or 6,000 people. The Ku Klux Klan are down to about 3,000 people. And the combined membership of all neo-Nazi groups are probably just 1,500 to 2,000."

In a nation of more than 270 million people, the small size of such fringe groups represents a tiny danger, yet they are the target of what Mr. Wilcox calls an "industry" of watchdog groups.

Robert Stacy McCain, *The Washington Times*, May 9, 2000.

There may also be found on the site a listing of "Hate Crimes" commited in 1999. Unfortunately the site is structured in such a way that makes it impossible to pull up the whole list. Having made a perfunctory examination of that list it revealed that tricks were used to inflate the numbers. The following acts are now "Hate Crimes": Having a Rally, having a Rally that was called off, meetings, and Un-described graffiti on a wall, a message chalked on a sidewalk, shouting a racial slur, the distribution of leaflets, false statement made about a non-existent swastika. Well it won't be long before Mr. Dees and co. will have their thought police review everyone's dreams to make sure that they are in compliance with their strange ideas of right and wrong.

We should at this point consider the vast amounts of money being diverted from real Christian charity to the poor and needy in order to keep Dees and co. living in the outrageously opulent style to which they have become accustomed.

Just exactly how large is the mom and pop hate mongering at SPLC? Their 1998 Income Tax Return shows net assets of $136,768,758.00. . . . The SPLC is one huge money machine, operating for the sole purpose of keeping Morris and f[r]iends in the high style of Living, and to afford him the funds for his numerous trysts. The palace out of which they operate in Montgomery. Alabama makes the average corporate headquarters look like a piker. Why do I call these people who claim to educate the public, schools, teachers and others about hate, a hate group? The reason is that they use hate as a weapon to induce innocent fools into giving them money. Consider that at 5% interest they would make an income of $680,000.00 just on their net assets. According to Randall Williams, a disgruntled ex-employee of SPLC, "Our donor base was anchored by wealthy Jewish contributors on the East and West coasts, and they gave big bucks. We were able to take in $3 million more a year than we could spend. Still Morris continued to send out fund raising letters about the 'Klan Menace' and the money kept po[u]ring in."

SPLC Is a Wealthy Organization

In a headline Feb. 13 1994, in the *Montgomery Advertiser* we learn, "Charity of Riches—they're drowning in their own affluence." The article goes on to explain that SPLC is raising so much money that they can not spend enough of it to keep their books on an even keel. In 1994 SPLC already had a $52 million cash reserve. They would be surprised how right they were if they saw that the cash reserve had grown to over $130 million, a growth of almost 300% in 1998. All this sort of makes me think that there should be an IRS rule about how much a 501c tax ex[em]pt corporation is allowed to retain as unused surplus; after all there are such rules for private corporations.

A close look at the SPLC indicates an organization that is essentially run for and by one man Morris Dees. Many of his avid supporters, some 600,000, see Dees as a hero. Since the bulk of his support comes from the Jewish communities in New York City, Los Angeles and Chicago, very far away from Montgomery, you can begin to grasp the reason for it.

Attacks by SPLC have been on numerous individuals under false pretence. Eustace Mullins is a well-known author and friend living in Saunton, Virginia. Now I am sure that there may be some people who disagree with Mullins but that does not make his publishing company, Revelation Books, a hate group. In fact, attacking an elderly author of dozens of widely circulated books and listing that publishing company as "Hate Group" is the act of hate. Mullins was a confidant of Ezra Pound who was the greatest American poet of the 20th century. The very first book he produced was at the suggestion of Ezra Pound; *The Secrets of the Federal Reserve* is considered the lexicon of all the books written on the FRS [federal reserve system]. How a publishing company with one sole employee, its author, constitutes a group is likewise never once explained. Far from being alone, the *Jubilee Newspaper* is listed under Identity whatever that is. How a newspaper can be classed as "Hate Group" is never explained, and the fact that it is a newspaper is omitted from the listing. I have no doubt that within short order SPLC will find some way to get my name on the list, because everyone who at one time or another criticized SPLC or Dees has wound up listed.

Phony Listings

As I have surmised, the entire listings are phony; it is inflated for one and only one purpose: to raise money and get unknowing people's support. Just consider some of the listed groups: American Nationalist Party, Christian Defense League, European American Education Assoc, Christian Bible Ministry, Christian Research, Land of Peace, and, yes, you guessed it *America First*. Who's missing? The Jewish

Defense League, The ADL [Anti-Defamatian League], the NAACP, the JDL, the WJC, NOW [National Organization for Women]. Like I said, if you're Jewish, Black, Hispanic, Oriental or female you couldn't be a "Hate Group" in Mr. Dees's lexicon.

How does SPLC get suckers to send them money? Well there's the Wall of Tolerance. It is to be constructed in Montgomery, Al. For a mere $35.00 your name will be listed on the wall. Or you can for the mere amount of $25.00 obtain SPLC publications for the next two years. Naturally, every letter, brochure, and flier tells the potential contributor that all payments are totally tax deductible. Then there's *Klanwatch* & Militia Task Force, who produces a brochure with lots of pictures including a photo of the Oklahoma City bombing, which was proven not to be in any way connected to any group. Then we have Teaching Tolerance as a program for schools and teachers, which is nothing, less than a concerted effort at multi-culturalism, one of the processes of destroying national [cohesion]. They sell programs to school systems. To date 50,000 of our schools have purchased this propaganda. Through the use of a very wide brush SPLC paints numerous political and social groups into their hate arsenal. Per example they use NEO- as a catch syllable to link different groups with whom they disagree. In Propaganda, that is simply called LINKAGE. Neo-Nazis, Neo-Confederates, and Neo-Conservatives are often linked in the same paragraph. Their most effective method of fundraising is through the use of specific letters on single topics to explicit groups. In this way Jews in NYC, LA and Chicago is their largest single contributory segment.

"Nature tells us to take care of our own kind and only our own kind. We do not regard any of the mud races to be our own kind."

Racial Hatred Is Necessary to Save the White Race

Matthew Hale

Matthew Hale is the Pontifex Maximus (supreme leader) of the World Church of the Creator (now renamed the Creativity Movement). In the following viewpoint he argues that the white race, which he claims is responsible for all that is worthwhile in the world, is in danger of being destroyed by people of color. Hale contends that the law of nature dictates that people must love and protect their own kind, which for white people means promoting white interests above those of minorities. According to Hale, white people should hate the "mud races" in order to protect their own race.

As you read, consider the following questions:

1. In what way is Christianity destructive, according to Hale?
2. Why does Hale single out Jews as special enemies?
3. How does Hale propose to change white thinking on issues of race?

W̲ho is the "Creator"?
     The White Race. White people are the creators of all worthwhile culture and civilization. Also, believers in our racial religion are called Creators.

If you were to sum up the objective of your religion, Creativity, in one sentence what would that be?

That objective would be: The Survival, Expansion and Advancement of the White Race.

Why is that so important?

It is a matter of priorities. Our religion is based on the ultimate of all truths: The Eternal Laws of Nature. Nature tells each species to expand and upgrade itself to the utmost of its abilities. Since the White Race is Nature's finest achievement and since we encompass the White Race, there can hardly be any other goal that even compares in importance.

As a rule, racists and anti-Semites reject those labels. You embrace them. Why?

Because the first prerequisite to our attaining victory is to be completely honest about what we are and what we are not. We are racists because we believe in Race. We are anti-Semites because we oppose the Jews.

Isn't your religion based on hate?

No, on the contrary, it is based on love—love for the White Race. Besides being based on the Eternal Laws of Nature, Creativity furthermore is based on the lessons of history, on logic and common sense.

The World Church of the Creator is often described with words like "hate monger," "hate organization," "hate speech." Is this fair?

No, it isn't fair since every organization—whatever it may be—hates something or someone. Since other organizations aren't labeled "hate" groups, etc., why should we be singled out like this? We don't exist out of hatred for the other races but out of love for our own Race.

But isn't it part and parcel of your religion to hate the Jews, blacks and other colored people?

True, but if you love and want to defend those whom you love, your own family, your own White Race; then hate for your enemies comes natural and is inevitable. Love and hate are two sides of the same coin. Only a hypocrite and a liar will go into battle against his enemies proclaiming love.

But weren't all the atrocities committed by Christians throughout history done by people who were not following Christianity's teaching of love?

Since these killings, tortures, and persecutions were carried on by the highest leaders and authorities of the various Churches themselves, such as the Popes, by Zwingli, Luther, Calvin, etc., we must presume that the teachings of Christianity, which at best are ambiguous, contradictory and hypocritical, must be held responsible for producing these kinds of people and this kind of insanity. But if we turn to the New Testament, we find Christ himself dispensing such hateful advice as, for example, in Luke 14:26: "If any man come to me, and hate not his father, and mother and wife, and children, and brethren and sisters, yea and his own life also, he cannot be my disciple." What idiotic and destructive advice!

Hate Your Enemies

What then is Creativity's final position on love and hate?

We follow the eternal wisdom of Nature's laws, which are completely opposite to the suicidal teachings of Christianity. Whereas Christianity says to "love your enemies" and to hate your own kind (see, e.g., Luke 14:26), we say just the opposite. We say that in order to survive, we must overcome and destroy those that are a threat to our existence; namely, our deadly enemies. At the same time, we advocate love and protection for those that are near and dear to us: our family and our own race, which is an extension of the family.

How does this differ from Christianity?

Christianity teaches love your enemies and hate your own kind, while we teach exactly the opposite, namely hate and destroy your enemies and love your own kind. Whereas Christianity's teachings are suicidal, our creed brings out the best creative and constructive forces inherent to the White Race. Whereas Christians are destroyers, we are builders.

What do you mean about Christianity being a destroyer?

Christianity teaches such destructive advice as "love your enemies," "sell all thou hast and give it to the poor," "resist not evil," "judge not," "turn the other cheek." Anybody that followed such suicidal advice would soon destroy themselves, their family, their race and their country.

If Christianity is as destructive as you say it is, how do you explain the fact that it has survived for nearly 2,000 years?

Smallpox has survived for longer than that, but the damage it has perpetrated on its victims has been devastating. Similarly, the creed and the church have survived for nearly 2,000 years, but the horrible damage it has wrought on the White Race is something else again. The Jews primary objective in concocting Christianity was to destroy their mortal enemies, the Roman Empire. In this they were successful beyond their wildest dreams. Two thousand years ago, before the advent of Christianity, the Roman Empire had reached an astoundingly high level of civilization, art, literature, law-giving, road building, language, and in dozens of other fields that are the hallmarks of progress in the White Man's civilization. Beginning with the reign of Augustus Caesar, Rome enjoyed two centuries of peace and prosperity (known as Pax Romana), the longest such span in history. As Christianity spread, and more and more poisoned the Roman mind, the good Roman citizens lost touch with reality and their minds meandered off into the "never-never land" of the spooks in the sky, fueled by fear of that humble torture chamber, HELL. The result was the collapse of the Roman Empire, and the White Race retrogressed into chaos, barbarism, and a thousand years of the Dark Ages. Poverty, ignorance and superstition were rampant. Like a monster, the Christian church fed upon and capitalized on these miseries. But the church itself grew fat and powerful. . . .

The White Race Must Be Saved

What do you believe in?

Creativity is the Eternal Laws of Nature applied to all aspects of life, including and especially our Race. In order to get the full scope and breadth of our beliefs, you must read and study *Nature's Eternal Religion* and the *White Man's Bible*.

What, in substance, is that belief?

The aim of our religion, briefly, is promoting the best interests of our race, the White Race, which we believe is the highest pinnacle of Nature's creation.

Do you have a "Golden Rule" in your religion?

Yes, we do have a Golden Rule in our religion, and it does

not coincide at all with the Golden Rule generally accepted in the Jewish-Christian philosophy. Our Golden Rule briefly can be summarized as follows: That which is good for the White Race is the highest virtue; that which is bad for the White Race is the ultimate sin.

Segregation Will Keep the White Race Pure

The possibility of the White race continuing into the future will be predicated upon various methods of segregation. Our global numbers are but a small percentage of the overall human total, and those are rapidly diminishing. We have no more genetic homelands safe from the savage. Without some form of segregation the White race is most assuredly doomed. We know this. Most of humanity knows this. The difference is that we have to care, because most of humanity, including most of the White race, does not. How, then, do we bring about segregation when many of our own people actually believe that our extinction, though they would never call it that, would be a good thing? What can we do when most White folks believe that integration means a happy melange of people? The One World, One People construct. These poor dolts don't seem to want to understand that even with the Great White Race amalgamated, there would still be races and racism aplenty, just no White race.

Among the many first things we need to do is to come out from the shadows. We must be confrontational, aggressive, and never surrender a point. We must boldly assert our right to exist as a distinct race. Our cringing from the very word White, has gone on long enough. We must cease to pretend that we have no enemies, and we must not be afraid to name our enemies.

Terry W. Phillips, "The Direction Home," www.vanguardnewsnetwork.com, December 3, 2003.

Don't you believe in the commonly accepted Golden Rule of "Do unto others as you would have them do unto you"?

No, we do not, and the reason we don't is that when you analyze it more closely, just like many of the other shibboleths of the Jewish-Christian Bible, the so-called Golden Rule does not make good sense. To quote some examples: We would not treat our enemies the same way as we would treat our friends. Our relationship to our employees would not be the same as to our boss. Our relationship to our children would not be the same as that to our parents. Our relationship to members of the White Race would not be the same as to members of the black race, for instance and we would not expect the same kind of response. The number of examples that could be quoted are endless, and on closer analysis, it is a completely unworkable principle. . . .

"No" to Charity

Why do you limit your interest in the benefiting of the White Race only? Aren't you interested in all of humanity?

Nature tells us to take care of our own kind and only our own kind. We do not regard any of the mud races to be our own kind. They may be sub-species of some common ancestor, or they may not. In any case, we regard the White Race as having risen to the very top of the human scale, with varying graduations of subhuman species below us. The niggers, undoubtedly, are at the very bottom of the ladder, not far above monkeys and chimpanzees.

But couldn't your program be more charitable and help the other races advance, while at the same time promoting the White Race?

The answer to this rather tricky question is a most emphatic "NO!" We have no intention of helping the mud races prosper, multiply, and crowd us off the limited space of this planet.

Why not?

In answering this question, we again go back to the basic Laws of Nature, which show that each species or sub-species has its natural enemies, and it is a cold hard fact of life that the most deadly enemies of the White Race are first of all the Jews, and secondarily, all the other mud races who are competing for food and living space on this limited planet. We have but two hard choices: (a) of either race-mixing and amalgamating with the mud peoples of the world, and thereby dragging down and destroying the White Race, or taking the course that the World Church of the Creator has chosen, namely, (b) to keep our own race pure and expand until we finally inhabit all the good lands of this planet Earth.

Wouldn't this entail a confrontation, in fact, a blood bath, in which the White Race might be wiped out?

Not necessarily. It is the program of the World Church of the Creator to keep expanding the White Race and crowding the mud races without necessarily engaging in any open warfare or without necessarily killing anybody. In doing so, we are only following the same principle as the colonization and westward expansion of America. During this great and productive epoch of the White Race, we kept expanding westward and onward by settling the lands that were occupied by an inferior human sub-species, namely, the Indians. It is true that there were some minor clashes, but there was not any open war of extermination. Had America not pursued this program of pushing onward and crowding the Indian, we would never have built this great stronghold of the White Race which we now call America. This is the real American way and we of the World Church of the Creator are expanding the American way on a worldwide basis.

Advance the White Race

But isn't this cruel and inhuman?

No, it is not. It is just a matter of deciding whether you would rather have your own future progeny of beautiful, intelligent White people survive and inhabit this earth, or whether you would rather see them submerged in a flood tide of mud races. In the latter case, all beauty, culture and civilization would vanish. The more we help the mud races to expand and multiply, the more we are robbing our own future generations of food, space and existence on this planet Earth. Furthermore, the mud races are doing to us that very thing in the present stage of history. They have viciously driven out and killed the White population in many countries in Africa, and I might add with the connivance and help of Jews and White traitors. Our Jewish-controlled Government right here in America is promoting the expansion and proliferation of the niggers in the United States, and shrinking the White population so that in a few generations practically all of the United States will be either completely black or mongrelized. It is strange indeed that the bleeding hearts who are so concerned about the survival of the mud races seem to be completely unconcerned about the mongrelization and destruction of the White Race, a process that is now going on before our very eyes.

But in your book Nature's Eternal Religion, *aren't you actually advocating the extermination of the Jews?*

Nowhere in our book do we ever suggest killing anybody. Our program simply is to unite the White Race for its own survival and protection, expansion and advancement. It is because the White Race has flagrantly violated Nature's Laws of looking after its own, and stupidly and foolishly instead has subsidized the expansion and proliferation of our enemies, the multitudes of mud races, that we are now on a collision course with disaster. We Creators strongly advocate that we stop this foolishness of subsidizing our enemies, and let them shift for themselves, and we take care of our own.

But wouldn't this mean the decline and perhaps the extermination of the colored races?

Perhaps it would, but that is not our responsibility, nor is it our doing. Nature has decreed that every species on the face of this earth be engaged in a struggle for survival on its own merits in competition with every other species. In no case, in no species in Nature, does the stronger and superior species voluntarily hold itself back and help subsidize a weaker and inferior species so that inferior species might crowd it from the face of the earth. No other species, that is, except the White Race, is foolishly engaging in that kind of foolish philosophy. We Creators say that this is suicidal and that we must drastically change our course. Every individual, sooner or later, dies anyway, but it is a matter of the survival of our own species, our own kind, that we are interested in. Since there is not enough land, food, and substance to support an ever exploding horde of mud races, the vital question as we stated before is: do we want our own kind to survive, or do we want the suicide of our own future generations in a world flooded by the sub-human mud races? . . .

Do you hate police and military personnel?

No. The United States Iron Heel's military and police forces are evil institutions, but we have nothing against many individual cops and soldiers, who are often the best of our Race. Indeed, many cops and soldiers are sympathetic to the pro-White cause.

Why do you use the term "niggers" in your books instead of showing some respect for the blacks and calling them "Negroes"?

This is a deliberate choice of words. As we state on page 42 in *Nature's Eternal Religion*, we must stop giving them credit and respect which they did not earn, do not deserve, and never did. Again, it is very strange that the same people who are so affronted by the niggers not getting their "proper respect" are totally unconcerned about the vicious, unwarranted attacks by the niggers and other mud races upon the White Race and will not lift a finger in the defense of their own kind. They seem to deem it quite proper that the niggers should be loyal to their race, the Jews should be loyal to their race, but when the White Man is asked to show a loyalty to his own race, he is immediately denounced, even by members of his own race, as being a racist, a bigot, a Nazi, and many other derogatory smear words that the Jews have concocted.

Jews

Why do you single out the Jews, who after all comprise less than one percent of the population of the world as your No. 1 enemy?

There are many good and valid reasons why the Jew deserves this special distinction. (a) The Jewish race, united through their Mosaic religion for thousands of years, has been for many centuries, and is today, the most powerful race on the face of the earth. (b) They not only control the news media, television networks, newspapers, and the money of the world, as of the United States, but through such power they also control the governments of the world. (c) They do, in fact, control most of the nerve centers of power in the United States and throughout the world. (d) It has been their age-old goal, not only for centuries, but for millennia, to pull down, mongrelize and destroy the White Race. (e) They have been very successful in doing this. We therefore conclude that they are a most dangerous threat to the further survival of the White Race.

Since you claim that your objectives do not include killing the Jews, just what do you propose?

It is our purpose to drive the Jews from power and eventually drive them from our shores back to Israel or whatever part of the world they choose to live in as a country of their own (perhaps also the island of Madagascar) without robbing other people of their established country.

How do you propose to do this?

By uniting and organizing the White race, and through the creed and program of the World Church of the Creator. By preaching and promoting racial loyalty among our own White Racial Comrades and making them conscious of their proud and wonderful heritage, we believe that we can mobilize the full power of the White Race and AGAIN REGAIN CONTROL OF OUR GOVERNMENT AND OUR OWN DESTINY. Once we have done that much, we believe that the fight against the Jews, the niggers and the mud races of the world is as good as won. Just distributing ten million copies of *Nature's Eternal Religion* and the *White Man's Bible* would put us well on the road to victory.

Didn't Hitler try to do the same thing and fail?

There are 500 million White people on the face of this planet. Organized and united they constitute an awesome power that would overwhelm the other peoples of the world, namely the mud races, in any kind of contest, or in any show of force. Whereas Hitler's program was similar to what we are proposing, we have learned from his failures and have made some significant changes. Whereas Hitler promoted and advocated pan-Germanism, namely, the German people as the core of his political movement, we, on the other hand, denounce Nationalism as an artificial barrier and a divisive force preventing the unification of the White Race. We promote and advocate the inclusion of all the good members of the White Race throughout the world, and propose to unite them in one solid battering ram under the banners of our religion. There are some other significant differences between our program and that of Adolf Hitler.

Why do you believe that a religious organization is a better means of accomplishing such objectives than a political party?

There are several reasons why we are convinced that we must have a religious base rather than a political party to do the job. (a) Religion embraces just about every aspect of a people's life—economies, morals, customs, law, government, education, eugenics, and above all, in our religion, the survival, expansion and advancement of our own race. (b) A political party, on the other hand, has a much narrower base. (c) Politics has a weaker appeal to an individual's loyalty. (d)

Religion, on the other hand, has a much deeper and profound influence on the entire course of his life. (e) Furthermore, history shows that religions can and do last for thousands of years, whereas practically any other human organization, whether it be government, nations, financial corporations, political parties, or whatever, are relatively short-lived, some of them existing for a few years or even less, and then fading from the scene. Of the thousands of political parties that have come and gone, few have lasted longer than perhaps fifty years and very few longer than a hundred years. In contrast to this, the Jews' Mosaic religion has lasted for several thousand years and been the keystone of the survival of the Jewish race, not to mention the horribly destructive ramifications in the lives and destruction of other nations. . . .

Changing White Thinking

What do you consider the main difficulty in winning your struggle?

The main problem we have is not overcoming the niggers and the Jews, and the mud races in general, but reeducating the perverted and twisted thinking that has poisoned the minds of the White Race over the many centuries. Despite the fact that the White Race is the most intelligent creature in the fields of logic, mathematics, science, inventions, medicine, and hundreds of other creative and productive areas, yet when it comes to the questions of race and religion, the White Race seems to be strangely stupefied as if under the influence of a mind-warping drug. And, in a way, the White Man's mind is warped as if poisoned with drugs. And this poison is the propaganda that the Jew has foisted on the White Race for all these centuries. The most potent of all these propaganda poisons that had infiltrated the White Man's thinking is the Christian religion. So, our main problem is replacing that religion with a sound racial religion for our own survival, expansion and advancement. As soon as we are able to straighten out the White Man's thinking, we can regard our problems and our struggle as good as won. Placing ten million copies of *Nature's Eternal Religion* and the *White Man's Bible* in the hands of our White Racial Comrades would be a major step in that direction. What a bargain that would be for the White Race!

How do you propose to "straighten out the White Man's thinking," as you put it?

This is the most difficult part of the task, but not at all impossible. After all, going back to Adolf Hitler, we find that he was highly successful in changing the thinking of the German people from one of communism, despair, and self-destruction, to one of vibrant creativity, constructive productivity, and re-establishing a highly constructive faith in their own people. We believe we can do the same thing for the White peoples of the United States, by widespread promotion and distribution of our books *Nature's Eternal Religion* and the *White Man's Bible*, and following that up with a strongly organized World Church of the Creator. If the Jews could organize the Christian church for the destruction of the White Race, surely the White Race can organize itself for its own survival. We can do it and we will do it!

Does Creativity believe in God?

When you ask that question, it is as vague as asking: Do you believe in "Quantity X"? There are a million different versions of "God." There is the Jewish version—a vengeful God interested only in the welfare of the Jews and repeatedly killing and destroying the Jews' enemies. There is the God of the Mohammedans, Allah; there is the "loving" God of the Christians. Women's Lib says God is a female, the niggers say he is black. Then there is the hocus-pocus about the Holy Trinity—that of the father, son and holy ghost all rolled into one. Whereas most of these versions were concocted by man to take on the image of human form, other versions like the Church of Religious Science say God is an all pervading spirit, like the ether, not in the image of man at all. These are just a few versions out of millions. Actually even members of the same religious denomination differ widely and let their imaginations run rampant. But there is not a shred of evidence to back up any of this nonsense. The sum total of all these wild proclamations is that nobody has any facts to substantiate their claims, and the sum total knowledge about any so-called God is zero. We Creators, therefore, reject all this nonsense about angels and devils and gods and all the rest of this silly spook craft. We go back to reality, and back to the Eternal Laws of Nature, about which the White Man does have an impressive fund of knowledge. . . .

Since Creativity does not believe in a Supreme Being, nor in a life in the hereafter, how can you claim to be a religion at all?

We have every legitimate right to that claim. (a) The constitution in effect prohibits any authority, religious, secular or otherwise, from delineating what is, or what is not, a religion. In short, if you claim you are a religion it is as valid as any rival religion's claim. (b) One of Webster's many definitions of religion is: "A cause, principle, system of tenets held with ardor, devotion, conscientiousness, and faith: a value held to be of supreme importance." Our faith resides in the future of the White Race and our values are set forth in *Nature's Eternal Religion*, especially the SIXTEEN COMMANDMENTS. (c) There are several major religions that are known as Nontheistic. Among these are Confucianism, Taoism, Buddhism, some sects of Hinduism, and many others. Although they contain much mysticism and hocus-pocus we don't indulge in, the point is that they, too, do not believe in a God, but rather are socioethical systems proclaiming certain moral values. Yet they have been recognized as religions for centuries, and rightfully so. There are other valid reasons why we rightfully qualify as a religion, but the above should suffice.

The Eternal Laws of Nature

What kind of religion would you call yourself?

Our religion is rooted in race, and based upon the Eternal Laws of Nature. We are, therefore, a racial religion and a natural religion. . . .

Since you do not believe in God and you do not worship anything, what is the purpose of your religion?

We have set up the loftiest and most noble goal humanly possible, namely, the Survival, Expansion and Advancement of the White Race. If the White Race isn't worth the dedication of our most ardent labors, what is? Niggers and monkeys? Imaginary, non-existent spooks in the sky? In Creativity, we have given the White Race a great and noble purpose in life. We have given the White Race a program for its own salvation and advancement for the next million years. We have given our own race a creed around which all members of our race can rally, regardless of nationality. Finally, after thousands of years of floundering, divisiveness and self-destruction, the White Race now has a meaningful constructive religion upon which it can build a better world for itself and its future progeny forever and a day. . . .

Don't you have faith in anything?

Yes, we most certainly do. . . . We have faith in the future of the White Race and its ultimate triumph. We consider that as the highest and most significant goal. The fact is we believe in anything that has valid and meaningful evidence to substantiate it. . . . We do not believe in a world of spirits and spooks and we most certainly do not believe in the Jewish Bible which was written by a gang of lying, Jewish scriptwriters. We believe "A SKEPTICAL AND INQUIRING MIND IS NO VICE. BEING GULLIBLE AND SUPERSTITIOUS IS NO VIRTUE.". . .

Since you say that the Jews occupy all the nerve centers of power, just how do you propose to drive them from power and have the White Man regain control of his destiny?

We mean to do this by building and expanding the World Church of the Creator until it penetrates the thinking and the heart and soul of all the good members of the White Race. As we have stated before, our biggest problem really is straightening out the thinking of White People. We believe that it can be done and it must be done, in fact, by building a religious movement dedicated to the survival, expansion and advancement of the White Race. We believe it is the only way that this tremendous task can be accomplished. It can be done, and it will be done.

Doesn't Creativity believe in helping others?

Yes, we do, but we are highly selective as to whom we render aid, love and affection. We most definitely do not believe in loving enemies, nor helping them. Among our enemies, we have the Jews and the mud races. We, therefore, believe in selectively helping our own kind, namely, our own White Racial Comrades. The White Man is the measure of all things, and we believe in looking at everything through the White Man's eyes, from the White Man's point of view.

The Bible Is a Hoax

Hasn't the Bible been pretty well proven by recent scientific discoveries and isn't the gap between Christianity and science rapidly deteriorating?

Most definitely not. The answer to both questions is a loud emphatic, NO! The gap between Christianity and science is as wide as the Grand Canyon. It is widening as science progresses in giant strides. The gap is irreconcilable and unbridgeable. A study of astronomy and the discovery of billions of other galaxies makes the idea of spooks in the sky a laughable absurdity. A study of geology makes the idea of a universal flood in the year 2348 B.C. a non-existent hoax. A study of Egyptian history also completely repudiates the story of the great flood. A study of authentic history further repudiates the so-called "history" the Jews have concocted for themselves in the Old Testament. Suffice it to say that the conflict is endless and an excellent set of books has been written on this subject. It comes in two volumes and is entitled *A History of the Warfare of Science with the Theology of Christendom* written by A.D. White. Unfortunately, it is now out of print and extremely hard to come by. . . .

The White Race seems to have done quite well in maintaining itself. Why are you so concerned about its survival?

The White Race used to do quite well for itself in the 15th, 16th, 17th, 18th and 19th centuries, but no more. In fact, as late as 1920, the White Race was outnumbered by the mud races of the world only in a proportion of 2 to 1. Today, scarcely two generations later, it is outnumbered by the rapidly exploding mud races of the world, by a ratio of 12 to 1. The United Nations, which is a Jew-controlled organization, gleefully reports that in another generation the White Race will be outnumbered on the face of this earth by a ratio of 49 to 1. A person has to only have an elementary grasp of mathematics to see that the White Race is now a very much endangered species, and will soon be either crowded into extinction or mongrelized into oblivion. Either way, the White Race will be gone, and with it also will vanish all the good things that it has produced, such as civilization, culture, art and all the other valuable attributes that we consider as contributing to the good life. The tragic and ironic thing about all this is that it's the White Man's ability to produce ample food, the White Man's technology, the White Man's medicine, and all the other valuable contributions created by his own ability, foolishly transferred to the parasitic mud races that has caused the present dilemma amid catastrophe. It is these valuable contributions of the White Race transferred to the mud races that has caused the latter's explosive increase. It is the unalterable goal of the World Church of the Creator to bring the White Man back to sanity and to again conserve his creativity and productivity for the benefit of his own race and his race alone. . . .

Racial Socialism

Does Creativity agree with Adolf Hitler in all respects?

Not in all respects. There are four or five major issues in which we depart from National Socialism. The main difference is we believe Nationalism, per se, was and is a divisive issue among the White Race. We instead espouse RACIAL SOCIALISM to embrace all the good White people on the face of the globe, rather than Pan-Germanism.

But didn't Hitler kill six million Jews?

No, he did not. This, along with Christianity, ranks as one of the biggest lies and biggest hoaxes in history. Privately, among themselves, the Jews published the growth of their total world population between 1938 and 1948, as increasing from approximately 16,600,000 to 17,650,000, an increase of over a million. This would be an outrageous impossibility, if it had been decimated by 6,000,000 during this same period.

If it isn't true, why would the Jews want to tell such a monstrous lie?

It has reaped tremendous dividends for them. Having worldwide monopoly of the propaganda machinery, they were able to put that lie across with little or no opposition.

What were the "tremendous dividends" for the Jews you speak of?

(a) It enabled the Jews who were the real instigators of World War II and the real culprits, to appear to be the victims, and arouse worldwide sympathy from the gullible and unsuspecting Gentiles, or Goyim, as they call them. (b) Through this world sympathy, it enabled them to loot the

Arabs of their lands in Palestine, and set up the bandit State of Israel. (c) It enabled them to loot the Germans with "restitutions" in amounts of as much as a billion dollars a year to the State of Israel. In short, this is plain blackmail and looting. (d) It enabled them to pursue a vicious program of destroying all opposition to Jewish aggression and take-over throughout the world. (e) It has provided them with a bonanza in tightening their stronghold on the peoples of the world in areas of finances, of propaganda, of governmental expansion and the spread of Jewish Communism.

So what do you propose as the answer to the Jewish problem?

The only total answer is for the White people of the world to unite and organize and regain control of their own destiny. This is the highest right in Nature. In order to do so they have to unite around something and that something must be a meaningful, significant and worthwhile creed that all the good White people of this earth can dedicate their lives to. This we have provided in the religious creed of Creativity as set forth in *Nature's Eternal Religion* and the *White Man's Bible*. In it lies the philosophy, the creed and the program for the salvation of the White Race for its own survival, expansion and advancement for all time. It is every White Man's highest moral duty to promote, advance and disseminate this lofty creed, not only for his own generation, but also to our future progeny for the next million years. Therefore let us dedicate ourselves to this noble task and go to work. . . .

What does "RAHOWA" mean?

It is our battle cry. Just as the Muslims have "jihad," we have "RAHOWA." It stands for RAcial HOly WAr.

147

"Whatever name you place on these [white supremacist] organizations, they are purely and simply evil. They foment hatred."

Racial Hatred Is Immoral

Doug Anstaett

White supremacist organizations such as the World Church of the Creator (now known as the Creativity Movement) encourage hate and violence against non-whites, Doug Anstaett maintains in the following viewpoint. He argues that the goal of white supremacists is total separation of the races, and if that proves impossible, they advocate annihilation of those who are different from them. Anstaett insists that decent Americans have a responsibility to condemn racial hatred whenever they encounter it because it is evil. Doug Anstaett writes for the *Newton Kansan*, a daily newspaper in Newton, Kansas.

As you read, consider the following questions:

1. In Anstaett's opinion, into what two groups do racists believe people should be divided?
2. According to the author, what types of people comprise white supremacy groups?
3. What does Anstaett report is the number one goal of the World Church of the Creator?

Hatred is not new in America. We saw it in the evil that hit Littleton, Colo., in April [1999], when 12 students and a beloved teacher died in a hail of gunfire before the two perpetrators took their own lives.

We saw it in the bombing of the Murrah Federal Building in Oklahoma City in 1995, which killed 166.

We saw it in the dragging death of a black man by thugs in Texas.

We've seen it in numerous acts of terror against those considered "different" for any number of reasons throughout America's history.

And now we've seen it again, this time in white supremacist Benjamin Nathaniel Smith's multi-state rampage in which he targeted minorities as victims, killing two and wounding at least eight others.

It's sad, but in the land of the free, there sometimes appears to be no real freedom for those who are different, especially racial minorities.

Ricky Byrdsong, a black former basketball star and Northwestern University men's basketball coach, was the first to be killed. He was playing with his children when Smith pulled out his revolver and killed him.

The second victim was a Korean student at the University of Indiana in Bloomington. He was simply taking a walk with friends.

Racists believe that people should be divided into groups that deserve to exist and those who do not.

White Supremacists Are Evil

Smith was a member of the World Church of the Creator [since renamed the Creativity Movement], a white supremacist organization that distributed anti-minority and anti-Semitic literature.

Whatever name you place on these organizations, they are purely and simply evil. They foment hatred. They encourage violence against those who are different. They seek total separation of the races, and if that's not possible, annihilation of those who aren't like them.

Typically, they are comprised of loners, losers and misfits—folks who just simply can't fit in to the mainstream of life in America.

According to the Associated Press, late last year [1998] Smith wrote a letter to the *Indiana Daily Student* newspaper.

"America," he wrote, "has become increasingly nonwhite and the constitutional rights of racial activists have increasingly been infringed upon."

Ramirez. © 1995 by Copley News Service. Reproduced by permission.

In April [1999], Smith appeared as a witness for the World Church of the Creator's leader, Matt Hale, at a hearing before a bar association panel. He said that at times he had "considered violent acts to achieve racial goals, but Hale counseled me to act peacefully."

"Our No. 1 goal is to straighten out the white man's thinking," he said. "We're the new minority being crushed left and right. We're in a life and death struggle."

Hale, the "church's" supposed ringleader, still lives at home with his parents and spews his hatred from a room in the basement. That's an interesting "church," isn't it?

Diversity Helps America Prosper

There was a nation that separated white from black for decades. We applauded South Africa when Nelson Mandela left jail and helped his nation throw off the shackles of apartheid.

America didn't become a nation to separate itself from others. In fact, our nation has prospered because it embraced its diversity and its differences.

Every decent American should condemn acts of racial hatred in whatever form they take.

Periodical Bibliography

The following articles have been selected to supplement the diverse views presented in this chapter.

Bill Bickel	"Inside the Mind of a White Supremacist: An Interview with Matt Hale," About Crime/ Punishment, October 9, 2000. www.crime. about.com.
Center for New Community	"State of Hate: White Nationalism in the Midwest 2001–2002," Winter 2001. www. newcomm.org.
CNN	"Lott: Segregation and Racism Are Immoral," December 13, 2002. www.cnn.com.
David Duke	"Is Russia the Key to White Survival?" *Duke Report*, October 2000. www.duke.org.
Sam Francis	"First, Anarcho-Tyranny Comes for the Extreme Right," *Vdare*, May 22, 2003. www.vdare.com.
Joey Haws	"Supremacist Groups Posing Greater Threat," *MSNBC News*, June 4, 2002.
Robert Stacy McCain	"Hate Debate," *Insight on the News*, June 19, 2000.
Northern California Anti-Authority (NCAA)	"NCAA Interview with Anthony Nocella," Red and Anarchist Action Network, April 26, 2004. www.raan.yardapes.net.
Terry W. Phillips	"The Direction Home," Vanguard News Network, October/November 2003. www.vanguardnewsnetwork.com.
June Preston	"Women Join Supremacy Fight," *Detroit Free Press*, September 11, 1999.
Dean Schabner	"Out of the Kitchen: Has the Women's Rights Movement Come to the Extreme Right?" ABC News, December 12, 2004. www.abcnews.com.
Ferris Shelton	"Hate Groups," Exodus Online, September 9, 2003. www.exodusnews.com.
Southern Poverty Law Center	"Militia Groups Declining, Racist Hate Groups Up," June 25, 2001.
Elie Wiesel	"How Can We Understand Their Hatred?" *Parade Magazine*, April 7, 2002.
Elizabeth Wright	"Free Speech for Some, but Not for All: The Reviled Matt Hale," *Issues and Views*, November 2000. www.issues-views.com.

CHAPTER 4

What Extremist Groups Pose a Threat Worldwide?

Chapter Preface

Twenty-first century extremist groups, especially those with political agendas, are either reviled as terrorists or hailed as freedom fighters—with the label entirely dependent on who is doing the labeling. Thus, the cliché, "One man's terrorist is another man's freedom fighter." Defining terrorism—and who is a terrorist—is crucial to understanding extremist groups, their goals and tactics. Though difficult, finding an objective, internationally agreed upon definition of terrorism is central to the struggle against it. Boaz Ganor, director of the International Policy Institute for Counter-Terrorism, a research organization that develops public policy solutions to international terrorism, insists that "without a definition of terrorism, it is impossible to formulate or enforce international agreements against terrorism."

Violent extremist groups often use an "ends justify the means" argument to win support for their activities. They claim that if they are struggling for peace and the freedom of their country, they can use any means necessary—including terrorism—and not be labeled terrorists. The problem arises when both parties involved in the conflict claim to be fighting for the same cause. For example, both Israelis and Palestinians insist that they are fighting for peace and the security of their land. Each side calls the actions of the other terrorism. Clearly whose claim to the land is more valid cannot be considered when determining which party engages in terrorism. In this case, as in so many others, the cause and justification cited by both entities are the same. The key to defining terrorism, then, is not whether the use of violence is justified. Another distinguishing element must be found.

Ganor argues that targeting civilians is the dividing line between a freedom fighter and a terrorist. The definition he proposes says that "terrorism is the intentional use of, or threat to use violence against civilians or against civilian targets, in order to attain political aims." According to Ganor's definition, only violent acts can be considered terrorism, the aim must always be political regardless of the motivation, and the target of the violence must be civilians. An objective definition such as this would allow the international community to dispassionately evaluate the acts of extremist groups to determine which constituted terrorism and which were legitimate freedom-fighting activities.

An objective, internationally agreed upon definition of terrorism would go a long way toward helping nations distinguish terrorists from freedom fighters. Authors in the following chapter debate which extremist groups pose a threat worldwide. As the case of the Israelis and Palestinians shows, judging whether these extremist groups are terrorists is impossible without a clear distinction being made between terrorists and freedom fighters.

"The . . . transcript provide[s] a full and revealing picture of Al-Qaeda, showing it to be the most lethal terrorist organization anywhere in the world."

Al Qaeda Is a Worldwide Terrorist Threat

Daniel Pipes and Steven Emerson

Al Qaeda, a terrorist organization with worldwide operational reach, views the West as the ultimate enemy of Islam, Daniel Pipes and Steven Emerson argue in the following viewpoint. They maintain that as an umbrella organization that includes many militant Islamic groups, al Qaeda represents a serious terrorist threat to the world, particularly to the United States. Daniel Pipes is director of the Middle East Forum, a member of the board of the U.S. Institute of Peace, and an internationally known columnist. Steven Emerson is a nationally recognized terrorism expert and the author of *American Jihad: The Terrorists Living Among Us.*

As you read, consider the following questions:
1. According to Pipes and Emerson, a victory over what country inspired al Qaeda to attack the United States?
2. What is the ideology that keeps the various groups coordinated by al Qaeda together, in the authors' opinion?
3. What is the basis for the authors' argument that al Qaeda operatives are best thought of as soldiers, not criminals?

Editor's Note: This article was written prior to the September 11, 2001, attacks on Ameria carried out by members of Al-Qaeda.

[In May 2001,] a federal jury in New York returned a guilty verdict against the four defendants accused of plotting the terrorist bombing, [in 1998], of the U.S. embassies in Kenya and Tanzania. The successful prosecution of these murderers represents a great victory for the United States, for the principle of justice, and for the rule of law. We are all in debt to the brave and capable prosecutors.

Operational Range

Unfortunately, the trial does almost nothing to enhance the safety of Americans. The Qaeda group, headed by the notorious Osama bin Laden, which perpetrated the outrages in East Africa, will barely notice the loss of four operatives. Indeed, recent information shows that Al-Qaeda is not only planning new attacks on the U.S. but is also expanding its operational range to countries such as Jordan and Israel.

In Israel, for example, bin Laden has begun to develop a network among the terrorists of the Hamas organization. Last year [2000], Israel arrested a Hamas member named Nabil Aukel who was trained in Pakistan and then moved to Afghanistan and Kashmir to put that training into practice. He returned to Israel with well-honed skills in the remote detonation of bombs using cellular phones, and was detailed to carry out terrorist attacks in Israel.

Perhaps the real importance of the New York trial lies not in the guilty verdicts but in the extraordinary information made public through court exhibits and trial proceedings. These have given us a riveting view onto the shadowy world of Al-Qaeda—though you'd never know from following the news media, for this information was barely reported. Tens of thousands of pages from the trial transcript provide a full and revealing picture of Al-Qaeda, showing it to be the most lethal terrorist organization anywhere in the world. They demonstrate that Al-Qaeda sees the West in general, and the U.S. in particular, as the ultimate enemy of Islam. Inspired by their victory over the Soviet Union in Afghanistan in the 1980s, the leaders of Al-Qaeda aspire to a similar victory over America, hoping ultimately to bring Islamist rule here.

Toward this end, they engaged in many attacks on American targets from 1993 to 1998. One striking piece of information that came out in the trial was bin Laden's possible connection to the World Trade Center bombing in New York in 1993. A terrorist manual introduced as evidence was just an updated version of an earlier manual found in the possession of the World Trade Center defendants.

An Umbrella Organization

The court evidence shows how Al-Qaeda is an umbrella organization that includes a wide range of Islamist groups, including Hezbollah (Lebanon), Islamic Jihad (Egypt), the Armed Islamic Group (Algeria), as well as a raft of Iraqis, Sudanese, Pakistanis, Afghans and Jordanians. Each of its constituent groups has the capability to carry out its own independent recruiting and operations.

The groups coordinate through Al-Qaeda's "Shura Council," a kind of board of directors that includes representatives from the many groups. The groups meet on a regular basis in Afghanistan to review and approve proposed operations. Most of them have maintained close relationships with each other since the end of the war in Afghanistan against the Soviets. They know each other well and work together efficiently.

We learned from the trial that when operations in one place are shutdown, the rest of the network soldiers on, virtually unaffected. Even if bin Ladin himself were to be killed, this Islamist network would survive and continue to expand, sustained by its ideological adhesion. Islamism is the glue that keeps these groups together, and fired up. The court documents also revealed that although bin Laden has had a leading role in formulating and paying for Al-Qaeda, the organization did rely heavily on state sponsorship as well. For example, Sudanese President Omar Bashir himself authorized Al-Qaeda activities in his country and gave it special authority to avoid paying taxes or import duties. More remarkably, he exempted the organization from local law enforcement. Officials of the Iranian government helped arrange advanced weapons and explosives training for Al-Qaeda personnel in Lebanon where they learned, for example, how to destroy large buildings.

Perhaps the most disconcerting revelations from the trial

Wright. © 2001 by *Providence Journal-Bulletin*. Reproduced by permission of Dick Wright.

concern Al-Qaeda's entrenchment in the West. For example, its procurement network for such materiel as night vision goggles, construction equipment, cell phones, and satellite telephones was based mostly in the U.S., Britain, France, Germany, Denmark, Bosnia and Croatia. The chemicals purchased for use in the manufacture of chemical weapons came from the Czech Republic.

A Global Islamist Network

In the often long waits between terrorist attacks, Al-Qaeda's member organizations maintained operational readiness by acting under the cover of front-company businesses and non-profit, tax-deductible religious charities. These nongovernmental groups, many of them still operating, are based mainly in the U.S. and Britain, as well as in the Middle East. The Qatar Charitable Society, for example, has served as one of bin Laden's de facto banks for raising and transferring funds. Osama bin Laden also set up a tightly organized system of cells in an array of American cities, including Brooklyn, N.Y.; Orlando, Fla.; Dallas; Santa Clara, Calif.; Columbia, Mo., and Herndon, Va.

First, we should think of Al-Qaeda not as an organization dominated by one man but as a global Islamist "Internet" with gateways and access points around the world. Second, Al-Qaeda has a world-wide operational reach. Especially noteworthy is its success in the U.S. and Europe, where it recruits primarily (as this trial showed) among Muslim immigrants. The legal implications of this fact are as serious as they are delicate. Clearly, this is a major new area for law enforcement to grapple with.

Finally, this trial shows that trials alone are not enough. In conceptualizing the Al-Qaeda problem only in terms of law enforcement, the U.S. government misses the larger point: Yes, the operatives engage in crimes, but they are better thought of as soldiers, not criminals. To fight Al-Qaeda and other terrorist groups requires an understanding that they (along with some states) have silently declared war on the U.S.; in turn, we must fight them as we would in a war.

Seeing acts of terror as battles, not crimes, improves the U.S. approach to this problem. It means that, as in a conventional war, America's armed forces, not its policemen and lawyers, are primarily deployed to protect Americans. Rather than drag low-level operatives into American courtrooms, the military will defend us overseas. If a perpetrator is not precisely known, then those who are known to harbor terrorists will be punished. This way, governments and organizations that support terrorism will pay the price, not just the individuals who carry it out. This way, too, Americans will gain a safety that presently eludes them, no matter how many high-profile courtroom victories prosecutors win.

"Al Qaeda attacks are more likely to occur abroad, but the danger of this group is being exaggerated overseas as well."

The Threat of al Qaeda Is Exaggerated

John L. Scherer

John L. Scherer asserts in the following viewpoint that while small-scale terrorist attacks may occur over the next ten years, major al Qaeda attacks are over in the United States and rapidly diminishing throughout the rest of the world. Thus, he argues that the worldwide threat of terrorism perpetrated by al Qaeda—including acts of bioterrorism—is exaggerated. John L. Scherer edited the yearbook *Terrorism: An Annual Survey* in 1982–83 and the quarterly *Terrorism* from 1986 to 2001.

As you read, consider the following questions:
1. Why does the author argue that intelligence agencies are unlikely to uncover impending terrorist attacks?
2. What is the author's opinion of reports that al Qaeda plans one hundred attacks at a time?
3. In Scherer's opinion, what poses a greater threat to the food supply than terrorism?

John L. Scherer, "Is Terrorism's Threat Overblown?" *USA Today Magazine*, January 2003. Copyright © 2003 by the Society for the Advancement of Education. Reproduced by permission.

The threat of terrorism in the U.S. is not over, but [the September 11, 2001, terrorist attacks] may have been an anomaly. Intelligence agencies are unlikely to uncover an impending attack, no matter what they spend on human intelligence, because it is virtually impossible to infiltrate terrorist cells whose members are friends and relatives. At least five of the 19 [September 11] Al Qaeda hijackers came from Asir province in Saudi Arabia, and possibly eight were related.

The U.S. was not defended on 9/11. As soon as the aircraft were hijacked, helicopters armed with missiles should have risen to protect coastal cities. Two F-16s dispatched from Langley and Otis Air Force bases in Virginia and New Jersey, respectively, were too distant to reach New York and Washington, D.C., in time. On a cautionary note, the penetration of White House air space by a Cessna aircraft in June, 2002, and by several other flights since the World Trade Center and Pentagon attacks, indicates nothing much has been done.

Although there will be small-scale terrorist attacks in the U.S. in the next 10 years, major Al Qaeda operations are over. Of the more than 1,200 people arrested after 9/11, none has been charged in the conspiracy. This suggests the hijackers did not and do not have an extensive operational American network. Some intelligence officials have estimated that up to 5,000 "sleepers"—persons with connections to Al Qaeda—are living in this country, including hundreds of hard-core members, yet nothing significant has happened in more than a year. The arrests in the Buffalo, N.Y., area back up the possibility of such sleeper cells.

Al Qaeda attacks are more likely to occur abroad, but the danger of this group is being exaggerated overseas as well. Members of Al Qaeda cells have been arrested in Spain, Italy, England, Germany, Malaysia, and elsewhere, but scarcely more than a score anywhere except Pakistan.

The Threat of Terrorism Has Diminished

The threat of terrorism in the U.S. has greatly diminished, but Al Qaeda and Taliban prisoners realize they can terrorize citizens merely by "confessing" to plans to blow up bridges in California, attack schools in Texas, bomb apartments in

Florida, rob banks in the Northeast, set off a series of "dirty bombs," and have scuba divers operate in coastal areas.[1]

A recent book on Al Qaeda states that the organization plans 100 attacks at any one time. This is nonsense. There have been a handful of small-scale attacks with fatalities linked to Al Qaeda since Sept. 11, nothing near 100. These include a church bombing in Islamabad (five deaths); the explosion of a gasoline truck and bus outside a synagogue on Djerba Island, Tunisia (19 dead); a bus bombing outside the Sheraton Hotel in Karachi (14 killed); and a bombing at the U.S. consulate in Karachi (12 fatalities). Three of these incidents occurred in Pakistan. In addition, Al Qaeda links are suspected in late-2002 bombings in Bali and Kenya. The claim by Sept. 11 terrorist suspect Zacarias Moussaoui of an ongoing Al Qaeda plot in this country is a subterfuge to save himself.

Al Qaeda had planned attacks in London, Paris, Marseilles, Strasbourg, Singapore, and Rome, but most of the conspirators were arrested a short time after the Sept. 11 attacks. Meanwhile, no one had hijacked an aircraft in the U.S. using a "real" weapon in almost 15 years, although crashing planes into structures is not new. The Israelis shot down a Libyan jetliner they said was headed for a building in Tel Aviv in the 1980s. A Cessna 150 fell 50 yards short of the White House in September, 1994. French commandos prevented a jumbo jet, hijacked in Algeria by the Armed Islamic Group, from crashing into the Eiffel Tower the following December. In the mid 1990s, terrorist Ramzi Yousef plotted to have his friend Abdul Hakim Murad fly a light plane loaded with chemical weapons into CIA headquarters at Langley, Va., or to have him spray the area with poison gas. A Turkish hijacker attempted to crash an aircraft into the tomb of former Pres. Kemal Ataturk in Ankara in 1998. With enhanced security on at airports and passengers on commercial airliners who will react to any danger, this threat has diminished.

Terrorists have attacked on holidays, but authorities are now especially alert on those occasions, and the number and

---

1. The Taliban is a fundamentalist Islamic militia that ruled Afghanistan until ousted by the United States in 2001. The Taliban government gave asylum to Al-Qaeda terrorist leader Osama bin Laden.

violence of anniversary attacks have lessened. Al Qaeda has never staged an incident on a holiday.

Bioterrorism Attacks Are Unlikely

Chemical, biological, and nuclear (CBN) attacks are possible, but difficult and unlikely. Only one has succeeded over the last two decades—the 1995 Sarin incident on the Tokyo subway. Thousands were injured, but just six people died.

There have been no CBN attacks with mass fatalities anywhere. Terrorist "experts" simply have thought up everything terrible that can happen, and then assumed it will. Terrorists would encounter problems dispersing biological toxins. Most quickly dilute in any open space, and others need perfect weather conditions to cause mass casualties. Some biological agents, although not anthrax, are killed by exposure to ultraviolet light. The Washington, D.C., subway system has devices that can detect biological toxins. New York has the highest-density population of any American city, and for this reason might have the greatest probability of such an attack, but it also has the best-prepared public health system.

The Threat of Terrorism Is Overblown

The response of U.S. policymakers to the Sept. 11 [2001] terrorist attacks is based upon an overestimate of the threat of terrorism, and ignores the lessons that can be gained from an interdisciplinary approach to the problem, according to some think tank experts who are analyzing the issue.

"I basically think we are really overreacting to this in a fairly large way," said George Mason University economist Roger Congleton. "I think it would be useful for the press and the government to be reminded that the risks are not as gigantic as we seem to have been encouraged to believe over the last year [2001–2002]."

Christian Bourge, United Press International, August 10, 2002.

In one instance, Essid Sami Ben Khemais, a Moroccan who ran Al Qaeda's European logistics center in Milan, Italy, received a five-year prison sentence in February, 2002. His cell planned to poison Rome's water supply near the U.S. embassy on the Via Veneto. This group had 10 pounds of potassium ferro-cyanide, a chemical used to make wine and ink dye, but extracting a deadly amount of cyanide from this compound would have proved extremely difficult.

Americans are rightly concerned about a strike against a nuclear power facility, but terrorists would have to get through a series of gates and fences, bypass motion sensors, and outfight a heavily armed security force to enter a containment building. Once inside the structure, they would need to know the exact sequence to shut down a reactor. An aircraft diving at a nuclear station would have to hit a small target, nothing like the World Trade Center buildings, which rose 1,400 feet into the air. Containment vessels are 160 feet high by 130 feet wide, and storage casks are even smaller.

Politicians have proposed creating a bureau to protect food from terrorists, but no one in the U.S. has ever died from a terrorist food poisoning. In fact, the nation has experienced just one instance of tampering with agricultural produce, when members of a cult contaminated several salad bars at restaurants in Oregon. The biggest danger to the food supply would be from salmonella, E. coli 0157, clostridium botulinum, and cholera, but careless handling and improper preparation of food are far-greater menaces than terrorism.

The Department of Homeland Security Is Unnecessary

There are 168,000 public water systems in the U.S. Some serve as many as 8,000,000 people, while others as few as 25. None has ever been poisoned, although there have been attempts.

The FBI may need reorganization, especially since its failures preceding Sept. 11 resulted from officials making bad decisions. It is well-known that in mid August, 2001, officials at a flight school in Eagan, Minn., told the FBI that a French citizen of Algerian descent, Moussaoui, had offered $30,000 cash for lessons on a flight-simulator to learn how to fly a Boeing 747. He had no interest in learning how to land the plane. Moussaoui was arrested three weeks before the attacks. One week before the hijackings, French intelligence informed the FBI that he was an Islamic militant who had visited Afghanistan and had links to Al Qaeda. FBI agents could have entered Moussaoui's computer and obtained his phone records using the Federal statutes already in place, but which were ignored or forgotten by officials.

Reorganizations refuse to acknowledge that some individuals are smarter and more knowledgeable than others, and new personnel will eventually resolve these problems. The new Department of Homeland Security will disrupt normal channels of communication and create even more bureaucratic confusion. It will compete for resources with the National Security Council and it will be costly trying to coordinate 46 agencies and, judging from actual terrorist events in the U.S., wholly unnecessary. Americans must remain vigilant, of course, but there is no need to raid the Treasury or turn the country upside down pursuing phantoms.

> "*The PLO must engage in terrorism in order to obtain financial and diplomatic support from Arab states.*"

The Palestine Liberation Organization Promotes Violence and Terrorism

Paul Eidelberg

In the following viewpoint Paul Eidelberg argues that Palestinian terrorism is not a desperate response to oppression but part of the Palestine Liberation Organization's (PLO) strategy to destroy Israel. He asserts that the PLO uses terror to gain recruits and secure financial aid and diplomatic support from Arab states, which seek Israel's destruction. Moreover, Eidelberg maintains that the PLO promotes terrorism as a means of psychological warfare to weaken the Israeli will and make Israelis more likely to capitulate to Palestinian demands. Paul Eidelberg lives in Israel and is a member of the board of directors of the Freeman Center for Strategic Studies, a pro-Israel research organization.

As you read, consider the following questions:
1. In the author's opinion, why did Yasir Arafat use schools, mosques, hospitals, and other civilian structures to store arms in Lebanon?
2. According to Eidelberg, what purpose does the PLO serve in the Islamic world?
3. How is terrorism used as an instrument of economic warfare against Israel, in the author's opinion?

Paul Eidelberg, "PLO Terrorism and Grand Strategy," www.freeman.org, April 2001. Copyright © 2001 by Freeman Center for Strategic Studies. Reproduced by permission.

[Israeli] Foreign Minister Shimon Peres wants to continue the policy of negotiating with [Palestinian leader Yasir] Arafat despite on-going PLO- [Palestine Liberation Organization] Palestinian violence. Prime Minister [Ariel] Sharon rejects this policy, or so he would have us believe. The present writer will argue that negotiating with Arafat is a grave error. To explain, allow me to recall an article I wrote about the PLO back in March 1985, almost four years before Arafat renounced violence in Geneva.

1. Like all terrorist organizations, the PLO uses terror to gain recruits. Terrorist leaders know as well as Hollywood move-makers that violence and bloodshed are alluring to no small number of men. They do not harbor a softheaded view of human nature.

2. To attract recruits the PLO must of course succeed, from time to time, in killing Jews, especially in Israel. Only by murdering Jews can the PLO obtain from Saudi Arabia the financial means with which to buy arms. Only by murdering Jews can Yasir Arafat's PLO obtain diplomatic support from the Moslem world . . . above all from Egypt, the creator of the PLO and the most steadfast champion of this organization's claim to represent the so-called "Palestinian people."

3. Unlike Western politicians, Moslem leaders think in long as well as in short terms. Jewish children in Israel eventually become Jewish soldiers. Murdering one is eliminating the other. No less a "moderate" than [the late] King Hussein of Jordan urged Moslems to "kill Jews wherever you find them, kill them with your hands, with your nails and teeth."

Terrorism Is Part of a Grand Strategy

4. Now let us go a little deeper. Operating under the leadership of Yasir Arafat, another "moderate," the PLO [then ensconced] in Lebanon used schools, Mosques, hospitals, and other civilian structures for storing arms and other military purposes. The object was not only to inhibit Israeli retaliation against terrorist attacks, say on Israel's northern towns and resort areas. To the contrary, Arafat surely knew that such PLO attacks would compel Israel, at some point, to strike at the PLO's civilian sanctuaries with the consequence of killing Lebanese civilians, but of thereby alienating Amer-

ican public opinion and triggering U.S. military sanctions. Viewed in this light, terrorist attacks are instruments of grand strategy, the subject of the next consideration.

5. It was said above that the PLO must engage in terrorism in order to obtain financial and diplomatic support from Arab states. If the PLO were to go [purely] "political"—and not merely for the purpose of wresting Judea and Samaria from Israel in preparation for a mortal blow [by Arab states]—it would self-destruct; it would be of use to no one. The Islamic world uses the PLO to keep alive American fear of another Middle East war. This fear aligns the United States with Egypt and other Moslem autocracies against Israel's retention of Judea, Samaria, and Gaza [as well as] the Golan Heights. I am referring to the key strategic function of the PLO. . . .

6. Consistent therewith, Islamic autocrats have foisted on the U.S. the fiction that the "Palestinian problem" is the "core" of the Middle East conflict. PLO terrorism serves to dramatize this fiction because nothing gains the media's attention more than violence. The short-term pragmatism of American politicians enables Moslems to pander to one of America's worst instincts: the belief in "quick-fix" solutions . . . for all problems. And what is the neat solution to the so-called Palestinian problem? Simply Israel's return to her pre-1967 borders. Within those borders, however, are 600,000 [now almost 1.2 million] Moslems. These Moslems are not only related by blood to the mythical Palestinians in Judea, Samaria, and Gaza, but they identity with . . . the PLO. This unpleasant but strategically significant fact is conveniently ignored by sheltered American commentators on the Middle East [to say nothing of Shimon Peres].

PLO Terrorism Is Psychological Warfare

7. Consider, now, the impact of repeated terrorist attacks on Israeli morale [and this was written 8 years before Oslo].[1] Moslem leaders know very well the value Jews place on a single human life. . . . [Hence] one aim of terrorist attacks

1. According to the 1993 Oslo Accord, Israel recognized the Palestine Liberation Organization and gave them limited autonomy in return for peace and an end to Palestinian claims on Israeli land.

against the people of Israel is to break down their will and per-severance, their political sobriety and national solidarity. Jew-ish realism may give way to Jewish wishful thinking: the . . . desire for peace may move softhearted and shortsighted poli-ticians to enter into unwise and dangerous agreements. Here PLO terrorism functions as a form of psychological warfare.

Many Palestinians Support Terror

Many in the Arab world either seek Israel's destruction or con-sider suicide bombings, shootings, mortar attacks, ambushes, and other attacks—aimed not only at Israeli soldiers and set-tlers but at civilians living within Israel proper—legitimate "resistance" to Israel's occupation of much of the West Bank and Gaza Strip. Polls show that Palestinian belligerence rose as the peace process collapsed. Israelis say [Yasir] Arafat's re-jection of what they considered a generous peace offer at the 2000 Camp David summit showed that the PA [Palestinian Authority] remains committed to terror, not diplomacy. . . .

Many members of the al-Aqsa Brigades [West Bank militia], including some commanders, receive paychecks from the PA for working in one of its security services. In the spring of 2002, Israeli troops said they had found documents in Arafat's Ramallah headquarters showing that PA funds had paid for some of the brigades' terror operations, and [George W.] Bush administration officials say Arafat's reported approval of a $20,000 payment to the brigades spurred the White House to call for Arafat's removal.

Council on Foreign Relations, www.terrorismanswers.com, 2004.

8. Terrorism is also used as an instrument of economic warfare. Planting bombs in Jerusalem cannot but diminish tourism, on which Israel's economy to no small extent de-pends.

9. Finally, reluctant as the free press may be [to] say killing Jews is a religious obligation for Moslems so long as Israel remains a sovereign and independent state, ponder the words of Dr. Abdul Halim Mahmoud, rector of Cairo's al-Ashar University, theologically and politically the most in-fluential university in Islamdom: "Allah commands Moslems to fight the friends of Satan wherever they are to be found. Among the friends of Satan—indeed, among the foremost friends of Satan in the present age—are the Jews."

To begin to fathom this venomous hatred of the Jews, let us cite Professor Abd al-Rahman al-Bazzaz of the University of Baghdad: "The existence of Israel nullifies the unity of our civilization which embraces the whole region. Moreover, the existence of Israel is a flagrant challenge to our philosophy of life and a total barrier against the values and aims we aspire [to] in the world."

Support for Israel's Destruction

Not the "Palestinian problem" but the "Jewish problem" is the core of the Middle East conflict. For Islam there is but one "Final Solution" to this problem, which is why all Moslem states support the PLO Covenant calling for Israel's destruction. . . .

It is hard for men of good will to take implacable hatred seriously, which is why Adolph Hitler was chosen *Time*'s Man of the Year in 1939.

Thus my 1985 article. Only a postscript is necessary. Sharon will either make war with the PLO or succumb to its minister in the cabinet, Shimon Peres.

"Let me be very clear. I condemn the attacks carried out by terrorist groups against Israeli civilians."

The Palestine Liberation Organization Condemns Violence and Terrorism

Yasir Arafat

Until his death in 2004, Yasir Arafat was head of the Palestinian Authority, the governing body established by the Palestine Liberation Organization (PLO) in the 1990s. In the following viewpoint, first published in 2002, Arafat claims that groups who commit acts of terrorism against innocent Israeli civilians do not represent the Palestinian people or their legitimate desire for freedom. He argues further that although Palestinians are oppressed by Israelis, no degree of oppression and desperation can justify terrorist attacks. Moreover, Arafat insists that terrorism will disappear once Israelis are willing to see the Palestinian people as equals and negotiate a just peace with them.

As you read, consider the following questions:

1. What is the Palestinian vision of peace, according to Arafat?
2. What does Arafat insist is the Israelis' purpose in attacking him personally?

For the past 16 months [since November 2000], Israelis and Palestinians have been locked in a catastrophic cycle of violence, a cycle which only promises more bloodshed and fear. The cycle has led many to conclude that peace is impossible, a myth borne out of ignorance of the Palestinian position. Now is the time for the Palestinians to state clearly, and for the world to hear clearly, the Palestinian vision.

But first, let me be very clear. I condemn the attacks carried out by terrorist groups against Israeli civilians. These groups do not represent the Palestinian people or their legitimate aspirations for freedom. They are terrorist organizations, and I am determined to put an end to their activities.

The Palestinian vision of peace is an independent and viable Palestinian state on the territories occupied by Israel in 1967, living as an equal neighbor alongside Israel with peace and security for both the Israeli and Palestinian peoples. In 1988, the Palestine National Council adopted a historic resolution calling for the implementation of applicable United Nations resolutions, particularly, Resolutions 242 and 338. The Palestinians recognized Israel's right to exist on 78 percent of historical Palestine with the understanding that we would be allowed to live in freedom on the remaining 22 percent, which has been under Israeli occupation since 1967. Our commitment to that two-state solution remains unchanged, but unfortunately, also remains unreciprocated.

The Palestinian Refugee Problem

We seek true independence and full sovereignty: the right to control our own airspace, water resources and borders; to develop our own economy, to have normal commercial relations with our neighbors, and to travel freely. In short, we seek only what the free world now enjoys and only what Israel insists on for itself: the right to control our own destiny and to take our place among free nations.

In addition, we seek a fair and just solution to the plight of Palestinian refugees who for 54 years have not been permitted to return to their homes. We understand Israel's demographic concerns and understand that the right of return of Palestinian refugees, a right guaranteed under international law and United Nations Resolution 194, must be implemented in a way that takes into account such concerns. However, just as we Palestinians must be realistic with respect to Israel's demographic desires, Israelis too must be realistic in understanding that there can be no solution to the Israeli-Palestinian conflict if the legitimate rights of these innocent civilians continue to be ignored. Left unresolved, the refugee issue has the potential to undermine any permanent peace agreement between Palestinians and Israelis. How is a Palestinian refugee to understand that his or her right of return will not be honored but those of Kosovar Albanians, Afghans and East Timorese have been?

There are those who claim that I am not a partner in peace. In response, I say Israel's peace partner is, and always has been, the Palestinian people. Peace is not a signed agreement between individuals—it is reconciliation between peoples. Two peoples cannot reconcile when one demands control over the other, when one refuses to treat the other as a partner in peace, when one uses the logic of power rather than the power of logic. Israel has yet to understand that it cannot have peace while denying justice. As long as the occupation of Palestinian lands continues, as long as Palestinians are denied freedom, then the path to the "peace of the brave" that I embarked upon with my late partner [Israeli prime minister] Yitzhak Rabin, will be littered with obstacles.

The Killing of Civilians Is Never Justified

The Palestinian people have been denied their freedom for far too long and are the only people in the world still living under foreign occupation. How is it possible that the entire world can tolerate this oppression, discrimination and humiliation? The 1993 Oslo Accord, signed on the White House lawn, promised the Palestinians freedom by May 1999. Instead, since 1993, the Palestinian people have endured a doubling of Israeli settlers, expansion of illegal Israeli settlements on Palestinian land and increased restrictions on freedom of movement. How do I convince my people that Israel is serious about peace while over the past decade Israel intensified the colonization of Palestinian land from which it was ostensibly negotiating a withdrawal?

But no degree of oppression and no level of desperation can

ever justify the killing of innocent civilians. I condemn terrorism. I condemn the killing of innocent civilians, whether they are Israeli, American or Palestinian; whether they are killed by Palestinian extremists, Israeli settlers, or by the Israeli government. But condemnations do not stop terrorism. To stop terrorism, we must understand that terrorism is simply the symptom, not the disease.

No Terrorism Has Been Committed by the PLO

It is also important to differentiate between Palestine Authority violence and terrorism. While the Israeli right-wingers would have us all believe that the Palestine Authority, or in particular certain factions and forces answering to Fatah and other leading PLO factions are responsible for terrorist acts, when asked to back this contention all they can point at are legitimate acts of self-defense, i.e. gunfights with Israeli troops and armed settler gangs. The PLO renounced terrorism in 1988, and virtually without exception has stuck to this renunciation. Palestinian soldiers and police have engaged in gunfights with Israeli soldiers, police, and settler gangs, but this is legitimate self-defense as is fully endorsed and allowed by international law. The very height of Israeli *chutzpah* has been the condemnation of the assassination of Minister Rehavam Ze'evi as 'terrorism' in view of Israel's current targeted assassination policy in the Occupied Territories. Vilification campaigns notwithstanding, there has been no terrorism committed by the Palestine Authority or the forces under the command of President [Yasir] Arafat.

John Sigler, Essays and Commentary on Contemporary Middle Eastern Issues, www.eccmei.net, February 3, 2002.

The personal attacks on me currently in vogue may be highly effective in giving Israelis an excuse to ignore their own role in creating the current situation. But these attacks do little to move the peace process forward and, in fact, are not designed to. Many believe that Ariel Sharon, Israel's prime minister, given his opposition to every peace treaty Israel has ever signed, is fanning the flames of unrest in an effort to delay indefinitely a return to negotiations. Regrettably, he has done little to prove them wrong. Israeli government practices of settlement construction, home demolitions, political assassinations, closures and shameful silence in the face of Israeli settler violence and other daily humiliations are clearly not aimed at calming the situation.

The Palestinian Vision of Peace

The Palestinians have a vision of peace: it is a peace based on the complete end of the occupation and a return to Israel's 1967 borders, the sharing of all Jerusalem as one open city and as the capital of two states, Palestine and Israel. It is a warm peace between two equals enjoying mutually beneficial economic and social cooperation. Despite the brutal repression of Palestinians over the last four decades, I believe when Israel sees Palestinians as equals, and not as a subjugated people upon whom it can impose its will, such a vision can come true. Indeed it must.

Palestinians are ready to end the conflict. We are ready to sit down now with any Israeli leader, regardless of his history, to negotiate freedom for the Palestinians, a complete end of the occupation, security for Israel and creative solutions to the plight of the refugees while respecting Israel's demographic concerns. But we will only sit down as equals, not as supplicants; as partners, not as subjects; as seekers of a just and peaceful solution, not as a defeated nation grateful for whatever scraps are thrown our way. For despite Israel's overwhelming military advantage, we possess something even greater: the power of justice.

> *"[Basque separatists] have been blamed for killing more than 800 people . . . making it one of the most feared organisations of its kind in Europe."*

Basque Separatists Promote Terrorism

Paul Sussman

The Basques, people who inhabit the Basque region in France and Spain, have long sought from both nations political and cultural autonomy. According to Paul Sussman, a writer for CNN.com Europe, the Basque separatist group ETA (Euskadi Ta Askatasuna) has engaged in a campaign of violent terrorism against the Spanish government for over thirty years. Sussman maintains in the following viewpoint that ETA is responsible for more than eight hundred murders and at least seventy kidnappings, plus countless bank robberies and acts of extortion. He argues further that ETA members have received training from terrorist groups in Libya, Lebanon, and Nicaragua, and that the organization has close ties to the Irish Republican Army.

As you read, consider the following questions:
1. According to Sussman, what is the English translation of "Euskadi Ta Askatasuna"?
2. The author reports that the Basque region straddles what two countries?
3. What has been the response of the Spanish government to Basque separatist activities?

For 32 years the Basque separatist group ETA has been fighting for an independent Basque state in northern Spain.

During that period, ETA has been blamed for killing more than 800 people, kidnapping 70 others and wounding thousands, making it one of the most feared organizations of its kind in Europe.

ETA, founded in 1959, stands for Euskadi Ta Askatasuna, Basque for "Basque Homeland and Freedom." It killed what some say was its first victim in 1968.

Since then it has waged a relentless campaign of violence against the Spanish state, targeting politicians, policemen, judges and soldiers. ETA's deadliest weapons are car bombs, which have caused numerous civilian casualties. In 1980 alone ETA was blamed for 118 deaths, and in 1995 it nearly succeeded in assassinating Jose Maria Aznar, then leader of the opposition, now Spain's prime minister.

On September 16, 1998, the organisation declared a "unilateral and indefinite" cease-fire, raising hopes that its campaign was at an end. ETA called off the cease-fire in November 1999, however, and 2000 saw a sharp escalation in violence.

Fiercely Independent

The Basque country, or Euskal Herria as it is known in Basque, straddles the western end of the Pyrenees, covering 20,664 square kilometres in northern Spain and southern France. Spain officially recognizes three Basque provinces, Alava, Guipuzcoa and Vizcaya. A fourth neighboring province, Navarra, is of Basque heritage. Separatists consider these four provinces plus three in France—Basse Navarre, Labourd and Soule—as the Basque country, with a population approaching 3 million.

The area has always possessed a fiercely independent instinct. The Basque people are the oldest indigenous ethnic group in Europe and have lived uninterrupted in the same region since the beginning of recorded history.

Their language, Euskera, which is spoken regularly by about 40 percent of Basque inhabitants, bears no relation to any other Indo-European tongue and dates back to before the Romans arrived in Spain.

Bloodshed and Violence Plague the Basque Region

Since ETA was founded in 1968, some 800 people have died violently in the conflict. Most—617—have been killed by ETA. Significantly, the vast majority of ETA-inflicted fatalities—572—have occurred since the death in 1975 of Spain's longtime dictator, Gen. Francisco Franco. This has happened despite a gradual devolution of powers by successive democratic governments in Madrid upon an increasingly autonomous regional administration in Basque country. "There is no essential difference in powers between those enjoyed by the current Basque government here and that of a Canadian province, especially Quebec," maintains Alejandro Saiz Arnaiz, professor of constitutional law at the Basque University in San Sebastian. . . . The main difference . . . Saiz argues, is "the cancer of bloodshed and violence that, in contrast to Quebec, makes the Basque regional autonomous problem so much more difficult to resolve."

Barry Came, *Maclean's*, October 27, 1997.

For many centuries the Basques of Spain enjoyed a strong degree of autonomy. In the Spanish Civil War, two Basque provinces—Guipuzcoa and Vizcaya—fought against Gen. Francisco Franco, while the provinces of Alava and Navarra fought for Franco. Under Franco's dictatorship (1939–75), most of the Basque region had its remaining autonomy rescinded. Its culture, people and language were suppressed.

ETA and its demands for an independent Basque state arose in 1959 in the midst of this suppression.

Kidnapping and Bank Robbery Finance the ETA

ETA has focused its activities on the Spanish side of the border. For many years France provided a safe haven for ETA members, a situation that began to change in the mid-1980s.

The organisation finances its campaign through kidnapping, bank robbery and a so-called "revolutionary tax" on Basque businesses—a payment that is widely regarded as plain extortion. No one knows how many businesses make these payments.

According to the counter-terrorism office of the U.S. State Department, ETA members have received training in

Libya, Lebanon and Nicaragua, while the group also enjoys close links with the Irish Republican Army (the Good Friday peace accord influenced ETA to call its cease-fire in 1998).

Active support for ETA is limited, and although no accurate figures are available, its membership is not thought to number more than a few hundred. It is believed to operate in small commando cells of about five people each. The party that many believe to be its political wing, Herri Batasuna (founded in 1978), rarely scores higher than 20 percent in local elections, considerably less than the more moderate Basque Nationalist Party (PNV).

While many Basques support independence—up to 40 percent, according to PNV leader Xabier Arzalluz—the vast majority of Basques oppose the use of violence.

The response of the Spanish government to ETA's activities has been two-pronged.

On one hand Spain has sought to accommodate the region's strong sense of local identity. Since the early 1980s, the Basque provinces of Alava, Guipuzcoa and Vizcaya have been recognised as an autonomous region known as Pais Vasco, with its own parliament and police force, and with Euskera as the official language.

Violence Continues

At the same time Madrid has cracked down hard on anyone suspected of being an ETA member.

From 1983–87, a shadowy organisation called the Anti-Terrorist Liberation Group (or GAL, from its Spanish name), was blamed for killing 27 suspected ETA members. This later proved to be a major scandal for Socialist Prime Minister Felipe Gonzalez, who was in power from 1982–96. One of his interior ministers served time in jail for his role in a kidnapping carried out by GAL.

In 1997, 23 leaders of Herri Batasuna were arrested and jailed for collaborating with ETA.

Despite the crackdowns and widespread public condemnation of its activities, ETA has continued its campaign of violence. Inaki Azcuna, the mayor of Bilbao, said: "We have too many attacks and not enough dialogue."

It is a situation which, at present, shows no sign of changing.

> *"While the political rights of the Basque Country remain denied . . . while the renovated tracks of fascism remain, ETA will keep on practising armed struggle."*

Basque Separatists Promote Nonviolent Political Change

Euskadi Ta Askatasuna

The Basques are an ethnic group inhabiting the Basque regions in northern Spain and southern France. They seek political and cultural autonomy. Euskadi Ta Askatasuna (ETA), the Basque separatist party, argues in the following viewpoint that violence against Spain and France is justified because the Spanish and French governments have failed to recognize the Basques culturally and politically. ETA insists that it has tried repeatedly over the past forty years to end its armed conflict with Spain, but Spain's refusal to give the Basques the autonomy they desire makes peace impossible.

As you read, consider the following questions:

1. What does ETA argue is the response of Spain and France to their proposals for a political solution to violence?
2. According to ETA, what has the development of Europe in the past few years shown the Basques?
3. With whom does ETA declare its solidarity?

Euskadi Ta Askatasuna, "ETA's Statement to the Institutions and Citizens of Europe," www.baskinfo.org, June 11, 2002. Copyright © 2002 by Baskenland Informatie Centrum. Reproduced by permission.

O n 11th June 1995, [Euskadi Ta Askatasuna, the Basque separatist party] (ETA) sent a statement to the European public opinion for the first time. In that document this organisation explained the contents of a peace proposal—known as the Democratic Alternative—that we had published some months earlier and we requested to put pressure on the Spanish government to force them to change their uncompromising attitude.

Seven years later, the Spanish government has been in charge of the Presidency of the European Union for six months. That period will finish [in 2002] with the meeting of the leaders of the member-states in Seville (Andalusia).

Spanish fascism, French jacobinism, the building of Europe and the Globalisation: the Basque Country [is] in a tight spot.

The conflict that sets the Basque Country against Spain and France continues. Despite the power changes in the governments of Spain and France, despite the important steps towards the building of Europe, there is no indication that both oppressive states will give up the colonisation and oppression we endure in the Basque Country.

On the contrary, the Spanish government has imposed a state of siege in the Basque Country: ban on newspapers, increase in the amount of arbitrary detentions, ban on political organisations and groups of the popular movement and the legalisation of savage tortures. Subsequent to the [Arab terrorist] attacks of September 11th, [2001,] they have tried to achieve the complicity of the European institutions. In addition, taking advantage of its economic power—as in the filthiest times of the Spanish imperialism—they had increased the pressure on the countries "under their influence". Nowadays, the fascism and the restructuring of the Empire are the main features of the Spanish policy.

Increased Repression

During these years, one of the only changes has been the high speed acquired by the renovated Era of the Globalisation. In connection with the undergoing worldwide economic transformation, the building of Europe is just another part of the puzzle. The creation of a giant market has hampered the development and establishment of a social Europe.

After having created and reinforced the economic foundations of the single European market, the leading powers have [taken] the place left to the citizens and started to build on it. The speed of the European process is being marked by the capital and their financial needs. The Europe of the citizens, Europe's social chart and the Europe of the peoples were abandoned a long time ago.

On the other hand, the gap between the citizens and the European institutions is widening, as they recognise too. To avoid it, the European institutions are taking some measures. Against the Basque Country and especially against all the popular organisations that fight for the rights of the Basque Country, the measures they promote are different: the Schengen Space for the police control, the Watson law and the right to veto of Spain and France. In return for political proposals for a solution, more and more repression; that is our reality.

Meanwhile, the Basque citizens still make up a group of second-class citizens, trapped in the institutional nets of Spain's parliamentary monarchy and France's republic. Our rights remained kidnapped; by "kidnapped" we mean a group of citizens free to say whatever, but whose right to decide is undermined within both political systems. Furthermore, according to a new law Spain is planning to adopt, the Basque citizens will not be allowed even to say what they think!

No Future for the Basque Country

The Basque Country has got no future in the current Europe of the States. Lots of majestic sentences, lots of "democratic" rights, but during the last years the building of Europe has just shown us clearly that we do not have the right to think and to act as a people. To prevent the Basques from acting as such, the republic of France uses its false grandness and equity and Spain the democratic label given by Europe for the last twenty years. In the modern reservation for natives they built for us, we are told wickedly we shall only be as souvenirs for the tourists and for the history books; in fact, limited rights that can only be used in a reservation under their control. Up to now, the magnificent future offered by all the governments in Spain and France to the Basques

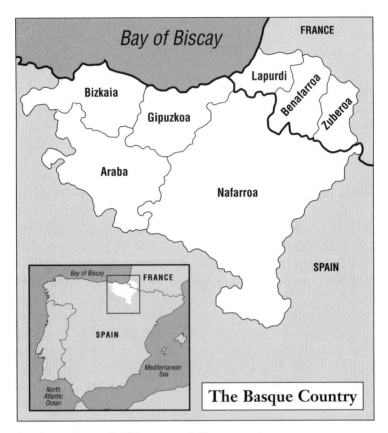

The Basque Country

has been that of a "democratic" segregation.

In addition, the republic of France and the "democracy" of Spain have built the future behind the Basque citizens' back; and, however, how many are the Basques who lost their lives in the Basque Country fighting in the resistance against the Nazis? How many are those who died in the war against the Spanish fascists? And, finally, we got paid, through their oppression and abuse.

The governments of Spain and France go against History.

ETA confirms its proposition to set the conflict on democratic grounds.

Concrete Proposals to End the Armed Conflict

ETA has usually said that there are ways to overcome the oppression and the armed conflict. Moreover, ETA has launched concrete proposals for the last forty years.

• In 1976, at the time the "Spanish democracy" was being born, the KAS Alternative [eight negotiating points for political recognition] was offered.

• In 1989, the talks in Algiers took place but the lack of political courage of the political party in power undermined the process.

• In 1995, ETA published a concrete proposal we called the Democratic Alternative [a negotiated solution to end violence].

• Later, ETA has left clear its goodwill to overcome the armed conflict through democratic ways in 1996 with a one-week initiative, or in the initiative of 1998.

In fact, we must assert proudly that ETA's strategic objectives remain the independence and socialism, but, at the same time, we make proposals linked to the reality to overcome the armed conflict. ETA will never speak in the name of our people. The members of ETA, instead of being terrorists, are a group of Basque citizens who are tightly tied to their society. Nowadays, ETA keeps on using the armed struggle in favour of the fundamental rights of the Basque Country. However, if those rights are guaranteed, ETA has repeated once and again that it will respect the decision of our people. The respect to our self-determination and to our territory. Both concepts must be guaranteed by a Democratic Process; that is the only condition demanded by ETA to overcome the current armed conflict. In fact, it could also be summed up in the slogan "Give the word to the People and respect it", the fundamentals of the Democratic Alternative. That's the only key to the problem. In addition, we must remember that in 1997, due to a campaign to become known [as] the Democratic Alternative, the judicial-repressive machinery of the Spanish government imprisoned the whole leadership of Herri Batasuna [the Basque left nationalist party]. So, what can we expect from the "democratic" propositions of our two neighbouring states? That is ETA's question to the citizens and institutions of Europe. At this moment in time, the juridical-political structuring of a new Europe is taking place; the European Institutions should know that the building of that Europe would be hampered if they were unable to reply with political courage to the existing conflicts and disputes. The responsibility would be yours too.

Solidarity with Oppressed People

[We are] in favour of a plural world and a fair society [we want to be] free to build the future. We would like to declare our solidarity to all the citizens who are worldwide fighting against injustice. . . .

ETA wants to confirm to the institutions, social agents and citizens of Europe its willingness to overcome the armed struggle. The Basque citizens should discuss, think over and say, without pressures, which is the Basque Country they want and which position in Europe they wish. While the Basque Country is doomed to die, ETA will keep on struggling. As ETA asserts its willingness to overcome the armed struggle, we also confirm that the only way against the obstinacy and arrogance of both oppressing states is the struggle. In any case, peace will only be brought by justice. While the political rights of the Basque Country remain denied; while the willingness to talk and negotiate remain deceitful; while the plans to ban the citizens' organisations, groups and initiatives continue; while there is no willingness to punish their use of torture and other atrocities; while the only truth is that of their despicable media; that is, while the renovated tracks of fascism remain, ETA will keep on practising armed struggle, as for the last four decades. Because the self-defence is our right. The struggle against injustice unites us, the dream of a fair society in the future too.

Efforts to Change

ETA requests to the European Institutions to make efforts to change the attitude of the Spanish and French governments. It requests to the social agents to come to the Basque Country, to meet all the agents here, to analyse the situation in its entirety and, in their working field to spread a view based on reality; because many media in Europe just transmit the view of the despicable Spanish media. We must take steps to set the conflict on democratic grounds. It is about time for each one to assume his/her own responsibility. ETA assumed its own one a long time ago.

Periodical Bibliography

The following articles have been selected to supplement the diverse views presented in this chapter.

David Bedein — "Your Taxes for PLO Propaganda," FrontPageMag.com, October 29, 2003.

Louis René Beres — "The Difference Between Murderers and Freedom Fighters," Freeman Center for Strategic Studies, January 29, 2004. www. freeman.org.

Michael Borop — "Focus: Basque Separatism," *World Sites Atlas*, May 15, 1999.

Christian Bourge — "Terror Threat Overblown, Says Expert," *United Press International*, 10, 2002.

J.T. Caruso — "Al-Qaeda International," Testimony before the Subcommittee on International Operations and Terrorism, Committee on Foreign Relations, U.S. Senate, December 18, 2001. www.fbi.gov.

Rod Dreher — "The PLO Man," *National Review Online*, April 3, 2002. www.nationalreview.com.

Michael Elliot — "Hate Club: Al-Qaeda's Web of Terror," *Time*, November 4, 2001.

Adam Entous — "U.S. Says Relations to PLO Tied to Terror Fight," *Miami Herald*, April 16, 2002.

Joel S. Fishman — "Ten Years Since Oslo: The PLO's 'People's War' Strategy and Israel's Inadequate Response," Jerusalem Center for Public Affairs, September 1–15, 2003. www.jcpa.org.

Reyko Huang — "In the Spotlight: Basque Fatherland and Liberty (ETA)," Center for Defense Information, May 23, 2002. www.cdi.org.

Kamel Jaber — "The Two Intifadas: PLO Activist Interview," From Occupied Palestine, November 4, 2003. www.fromoccupiedpalestine.org.

NewsMax.com — "Terrorism Nuclear Threat Real," February 1, 2002. www.newsmax.com.

Daniel Pipes — "Arafat's Suicide Factory," *New York Post*, December 9, 2001.

Republican Study Committee — "Tactics of Palestine Terrorism," September 11, 2003. www.house.gov/burton/RSC.

James Ridgeway	"Al Qaeda Duped?" *Village Voice*, November 16, 2001.
Lara Sukhtian	"PLO Taps New Prime Minister," *Washington Times*, September 8, 2003.
Time International	"Fear and Loathing Return: After a Long Truce, Spain's Basque Terrorists Resume Their Attempts to Bomb Their Way to Independence," January 31, 2000.
Wall Street Journal	"Iraq and al Qaeda," September 22, 2003.

For Further Discussion

Chapter 1

1. Matthew C. Ogilvie insists that racists use religion to justify their hate and violence. David Ostendorf maintains that the positive power of religion is the best weapon against bigotry. In your opinion, is religion a force for good or evil? Explain, citing from the viewpoints.

2. David Horowitz argues that Islamic fundamentalist groups on American college campuses pose a serious threat because they promote an anti-American agenda and lure students into terrorist activities. Shibley Telhami insists that most Arab and Muslim Americans were horrified by the Arab terrorist attacks on September 11, 2001, and are loyal to the United States. In your opinion, which argument is stronger?

3. The religious Right's notion of the United States as a Christian theocracy has no historical basis, according to Frederick Clarkson. He argues further that it is part of a harmful agenda that includes a variety of social and political issues. Norman Podhoretz, however, insists that there is nothing to fear from the religious Right because the group now embraces diverse religious views. In your opinion, which author is more convincing?

4. The Jewish Defense League insists that Jewish people have a right to use force and violence to defend themselves against threats from Nazis and other anti-Semitic groups. Angela Valkyrie claims that the Jewish Defense League is a violent terrorist group that threatens European Americans without provocation. Are there always other options besides violence to fight oppression and injustice? Explain, citing from the viewpoints.

Chapter 2

1. Fredrick K. Goodwin and Adrian R. Morrison argue that when radical animal rights groups harass scientists, they have a devastating effect on scientific creativity and medical research. Noel Molland, however, claims that violent action by radical animal rights groups is justified because peaceful methods do not get results. In your opinion, is using illegal means to achieve a noble goal ever justified? Explain.

2. Brian Paterson insists that socialism encourages violence and uses force to achieve its end of income redistribution. John Fisher argues that socialism is the cure for the violence and de-

structiveness of capitalism. Which argument is more persuasive? Cite from the viewpoints in your answer.

3. Brad Knickerbocker argues that radical environmentalists are terrorists. Emily Kumpel claims that ecoterrorism is sometimes necessary because it gets results. In your opinion, will the violent actions of radical environmental groups make the general public more or less sympathetic to environmentalism in general? Explain.

Chapter 3

1. Carol Rowan argues that white supremacist groups are violent and dangerous. Adrian H. Krieg, however, insists that the size of white supremacist organizations and the danger they pose is exaggerated by watchdog groups to encourage contributions from rich liberals. Which argument is more persuasive? Why?

2. Matthew Hale claims that it is permissible to hate non-Christians and nonwhites because they will ultimately destroy the white race. Doug Anstaett argues that white supremacist groups are evil and should be opposed by decent Americans. In your opinion, can a person be a decent American and still hate non-Christians and nonwhites? Explain, citing from the viewpoints.

Chapter 4

1. Daniel Pipes and Steven Emerson argue that al Qaeda is the most lethal terrorist organization in the world and a threat to all non-Islamic nations. They maintain that al Qaeda's acts of terrorism must be treated as wartime battles not crimes. John L. Scherer, however, insists that the threat of al Qaeda is exaggerated and that reasonable vigilance will provide adequate safety. In your opinion, which is more dangerous—overreacting to threats of terrorism or underreacting? Explain.

2. Paul Eidelberg asserts that the PLO promotes violence and terrorism as part of its strategy to destroy Israel. Yasir Arafat insists that the PLO condemns terrorism and the killing of innocent civilians and wants only peace and justice. Eidelberg is an Israeli and Arafat is the head of the Palestinian Authority. In your opinion, how does each author's nationality affect his argument?

3. Paul Sussman maintains that the ETA is a terrorist group that uses murder, kidnapping, and bank robbery to achieve its goal of a free Basque state and is unlikely to stop its violent approach. ETA argues that its violence is justified because Spain and France have failed to recognize the Basques culturally and politically. Further, ETA insists that it would stop its attacks if the Spanish government would end its repressive policies. In your opinion, is terrorism justifiable in the fight for freedom? Explain.

Organizations to Contact

The editors have compiled the following list of organizations concerned with the issues debated in this book. The descriptions are derived from materials provided by the organizations. All have publications or information available for interested readers. The list was compiled on the date of publication of the present volume; names, addresses, phone and fax numbers, and e-mail and Internet addresses may change. Be aware that many organizations take several weeks or longer to respond to inquiries, so allow as much time as possible.

American-Arab Anti-Discrimination Committee
4201 Connecticut Ave. NW, Suite 300, Washington, DC 20008
(202) 244-2990 • fax: (202) 244-3196
e-mail: adc@adc.org • Web site: www.adc.org

The committee fights anti-Arab stereotyping in the media and discrimination and hate crimes against Arab Americans. It publishes a series of issue papers and a number of books, including the two-volume *Taking Root/Bearing Fruit: The Arab-American Experience.*

American Civil Liberties Union (ACLU)
125 Broad St., 18th Fl., New York, NY 10004
(212) 549-2585
e-mail: aclu@aclu.org • Web site: www.aclu.org

The ACLU is a national organization that works to defend Americans' civil rights guaranteed in the U.S. Constitution. The ACLU publishes the semiannual newsletter *Civil Liberties Alert* as well as the briefing papers "Hate Speech on Campus" and "Racial Justice."

B'nai B'rith Canada
15 Hove St., Toronto, ON M3H 4Y8 Canada
(416) 633-6224 • fax: (416) 630-2159
e-mail: bnb@bnaibrith.ca • Web site: www.bnaibrith.ca

Affiliated with the American Anti-Defamation League, this organization works to stop the defamation of Jews and to ensure fair treatment for all Canadian citizens. It monitors violent extremist groups and advocates antiterrorism measures in Canada, and it publishes the annual *Review of Anti-Semitism in Canada.*

Center for Democratic Renewal
PO Box 50469, Atlanta, GA 30302
(404) 221-0025 • fax: (404) 221-0045
e-mail: info@cdr.org • Web site: www.thecdr.org

Formerly known as the National Anti-Klan Network, this non-profit organization monitors hate group activity and white supremacist activity in America and opposes bias-motivated violence. It publishes the bimonthly *Monitor* magazine, the report *The Fourth Wave: A Continuing Conspiracy to Burn Black Churches*, and the book *When Hate Groups Come to Town*.

Christian Coalition of America

PO Box 37030, Washington, DC 20003
(202) 479-6900 • fax: (202) 479-4260
e-mail: coalition@cc.org • Web site: www.cc.org

The Christian Coalition was founded in 1989 to give Christians a voice in government. The organization's goals include strengthening the family, protecting innocent human life, and protecting religious freedom.

Communist Party USA

235 W. Twenty-third St., New York, NY 10011
(212) 989-4994 • fax: (212) 229-1713
e-mail: CPUSA@cpusa.org • Web site: www.cpusa.org

The Communist Party USA is a Marxist-Leninist working-class party that unites black, brown, and white, men and women, and youth and seniors. The party speaks from a working-class perspective and supports labor and all militant movements for social progress. The Communist Party USA publishes the periodical *People's Weekly World*.

Council on American-Islamic Relations (CAIR)

453 New Jersey Ave. SE, Washington, DC 20005
(202) 488-8787 • fax: (202) 488-0833
e-mail: cair@cair-net.org • Web site: www.cair-net.org

CAIR is a nonprofit membership organization dedicated to presenting an Islamic perspective on public policy issues and to challenging the misrepresentation of Islam and Muslims. It fights discrimination against Muslims in America and lobbies political leaders on issues related to Islam and Muslims. Its publications include the quarterly newsletter *CAIR News* as well as the periodic *Action Alert*.

Earth First!

PO Box 20, Arcata, CA 95518
(707) 825-6598
e-mail: greg@EarthFirst.org • Web site: www.earthfirst.org

Earth First! believes that the earth's ecology has become seriously degraded and advocates direct action in order to stop the destruction of the environment. The organization publishes the *Earth First! Journal*.

Greenpeace USA
702 H St. NW, Suite 300, Washington, DC
(202) 462-1177 • fax: (202) 462-4507
e-mail: greenpeaceusa@wdc.greenpeace.org
Web site: www.greenpeace.org

This international environmental organization consists of conservationists who believe that verbal protests against threats to the environment are inadequate and advocates direct action instead. It publishes the quarterly newsletter *Greenpeace* and periodic *Greenpeace Reports*.

Jewish Defense League (JDL)
PO Box 480370, Los Angeles, CA 90048
(818) 980-8535 • fax: (781) 634-0338
e-mail: jdljdl@aol.com • Web site: www.jdl.org

The league is an activist organization that works to raise awareness of anti-Semitism and the neo-Nazi movement. The JDL Web site features news and updates on hate groups and activism as well as information on Jewish culture.

National Association for the Advancement of Colored People (NAACP)
4805 Mt. Hope Dr., Baltimore, MD 21215-3297
(877) NAACP-98 • fax: (410) 486-9255
e-mail: washingtonbureau@naacpnet.org
Web site: www.naacp.org

The NAACP is the oldest and largest civil rights organization in the United States. Its principal objective is to ensure the political, educational, social, and economic equality of minorities. It publishes the magazine *Crisis* ten times a year as well as a variety of newsletters, books, and pamphlets.

People for the American Way Foundation
2000 M St. NW, Suite 400, Washington, DC 20036
(800) 326-7329
e-mail: pfaw@pfaw.org • Web site: www.pfaw.org

People for the American Way Foundation opposes the political agenda of the religious Right. Through public education, lobbying, and legal advocacy, the foundation works to defend equal rights.

The foundation publishes *Hostile Climate*, a report detailing intolerant incidents directed against gays and lesbians, and organizes the Students Talk About Race (STAR) program, which trains college students to lead high school discussions on intergroup relations.

People for the Ethical Treatment of Animals (PETA)
501 Front St., Norfolk, VA 23510
(757) 622-7382 • fax: (757) 622-0457
e-mail: info@peta.org • Web site: www.peta-online.org
An international animal rights organization, PETA is dedicated to establishing and protecting the rights of all animals. It focuses on four areas: factory farms, research laboratories, the fur trade, and the entertainment industry. PETA promotes public education, cruelty investigations, animal rescue, and celebrity videos, and it publishes *Animal Times, Grrr!* (a magazine for children), various fact sheets, brochures, and flyers.

Prejudice Institute
2743 Maryland Ave., Baltimore, MD 21218
(410) 243-6987
e-mail: prejinst@aol.com • Web site: www.prejudiceinstitute.org
The Prejudice Institute is a national research center concerned with violence and intimidation motivated by prejudice. It conducts research, supplies information on model programs and legislation, and provides education and training to combat prejudicial violence. The Prejudice Institute publishes research reports, bibliographies, and the quarterly newsletter *Forum*.

Southern Poverty Law Center/Klanwatch Project
400 Washington Ave., Montgomery, AL 36102
(334) 956-8200
Web site: www.splcenter.org
The center litigates civil cases to protect the rights of poor people, particularly when those rights are threatened by white supremacist groups. The affiliated Klanwatch Project and the Militia Task Force collect data on white supremacist groups and militias and promote the adoption and enforcement by states of antiparamilitary training laws. The center publishes numerous books and reports as well as the monthly *Klanwatch Intelligence Report*.

Washington Institute for Near East Policy
1828 L St. NW, Washington, DC 20036
(202) 452-0650 • fax: (202) 223-5364
e-mail: info@washingtoninstitute.org
Web site: www.washingtoninstitute.org

The institute is an independent nonprofit research organization that provides information and analysis on the Middle East and U.S. policy in that region. It publishes numerous books, monographs, and reports on regional politics, security, and economics, including *Vision of the West, Hamas: The Fundamentalist Challenge to the PLO, Democracy and Arab Political Culture, Iran's Challenge to the West, Radical Middle East States and U.S. Policy,* and *Democracy in the Middle East: Defining the Challenge.*

Bibliography of Books

Linda Jacobs Altman — *Hate and Racist Groups: A Hot Issue.* Berkeley Heights, NJ: Enslow Publishers, 2001.

Wayne Anderson — *The ETA: Spain's Basque Terrorists.* New York: Rosen Publishing Group, 2002.

Jillian Becker — *The PLO: The Rise and Fall of the Palestine Liberation Organization.* New York: St. Martin's Press, 2000.

Chip Berlet — *Right-Wing Populism in America: Too Close for Comfort.* New York: Guilford Press, 2000.

Kimberly Blaker, ed. — *The Fundamentals of Extremism: The Christian Right in America.* New Boston, MI: New Boston Books, 2003.

Kathleen Blee — *Inside Organized Racism: Women in the Hate Movement.* Berkeley and Los Angeles: University of California Press, 2002.

Ruth Murry Brown — *For a Christian America: A History of the Religious Right.* Amherst, NY: Prometheus Books, 2002.

Steven P. Brown — *Trumping Religion: The New Christian Right, the Free Speech Clause, and the Courts.* Tuscaloosa: University of Alabama Press, 2002.

Jason Burke — *Al-Qaeda: Casting a Shadow of Terror.* New York: I.B. Tauris, 2002.

Ann Burlein — *Lift High the Cross: Where White Supremacy and the Christian Right Converge.* Durham, NC: Duke University Press, 2002.

Jane Corbin — *The Base: In Search of the Terror Network That Shook the World.* New York: Simon and Schuster, 2002.

Jane Corbin — *Al-Qaeda: In Search of the Terror Network That Threatens the World.* New York: Thunder's Mouth Press/Nation Books, 2003.

Mark Gabriel — *Islam and Terrorism: What the Quran Really Teaches About Christianity, Violence, and the Goals of the Islamic Jihad.* Lake Mary, FL: Charisma House, 2002.

Ann Heinrichs — *The Ku Klux Klan: A Hooded Brotherhood.* Chanhassen, MN: Child's World, 2003.

Brian Innes — *International Terrorism.* Broomall, PA: Mason Crest, 2003.

Eric Katz et al., eds. — *Beneath the Surface: Critical Essays in the Philosophy of Deep Ecology.* Cambridge, MA: MIT Press, 2000.

Andrew Kimbrell	*The Fatal Harvest Reader: The Tragedy of Industrial Agriculture*. Washington, DC: Foundation for Deep Ecology/Island Press, 2002.
Elinor Langer	*A Hundred Little Hitlers: The Death of a Black Man, the Trial of a White Racist, and the Rise of the Neo-Nazi Movement in America*. New York: Metropolitan Books, 2003.
Wayne K. LaPierre	*Guns, Freedom, and Terrorism*. Nashville, TN: WND Books, 2003.
Seymour Martin Lipset	*It Didn't Happen Here: Why Socialism Failed in the United States*. New York: Norton, 2000.
Joshua Muravchik	*Heaven on Earth: The Rise and Fall of Socialism*. San Francisco: Encounter Books, 2002.
Simon Reeve	*The New Jackals: Ramzi Yousef, Osama bin Laden, and the Future of Terrorism*. Evanston, IL: Northwestern University Press, 1999.
Mark Rowlands	*Animals Like Us*. New York: Verso, 2002.
Matthew Scully	*Dominion: The Power of Man, the Suffering of Animals, and the Call of Mercy*. New York: St Martin's Press, 2002.
Kim Stallwood, ed.	*A Primer on Animal Rights: Leading Experts Write About Cruelty and Exploitation*. New York: Lantern Books, 2002.
Carol M. Swain	*The New White Nationalism in America: Its Challenge to Integration*. New York: Cambridge University Press, 2002.
Carol M. Swain and Russ Nieli, eds.	*Contemporary Voices of White Nationalism*. New York: Cambridge University Press, 2003.
Jerome Walters	*One Aryan Nation Under God: How Religious Extremists Use the Bible to Justify Their Actions*. Naperville, IL: Sourcebooks, 2001.
Stephen D. Wayne and Clyde Wilcox, eds.	*The Election of the Century and What It Tells Us About the Future of American Politics*. Armonk, NY: M.E. Sharpe, 2002.
James Weinstein	*The Long Detour: The History and Future of the American Left*. Boulder, CO: Westview Press, 2003.
David P. Workman	*PETA Files: The Dark Side of Animal Rights*. Bellevue, WA: Merril Press, 2003.

Index

on love of Jewry, 59
terrorist activities by, 66–67
threat of, 64
on unity and discipline, 61
violence by, 65
  changing image of Jews and, 61
  is sometimes necessary, 60
Jews
  PLO psychological warfare against,
    169–70
  PLO violence against, 168
  white supremacists on, 139–41, 144,
    146–47
Jones, Bob, 21

Kahane, Meir, 59, 60, 64–65, 66
Kaiser, Kirsten, 116
Kansas Ecumenical Ministries, 31
Kenya, 157
Khemais, Essid Sami Ben, 164–65
Knickerbocker, Brad, 100
Krieg, Adrian H., 122
Krugel, Earl, 64
Kumpel, Emily, 105

Lee, Ronnie, 84, 90, 91–92
liberalism, 23–24
Locke, Edwin A., 95

Mackay, John, 21
Mainstream Coalition, 31
Marx, Karl, 26
McCain, John, 53
McCain, Robert Stacy, 127
McKibben, Bill, 106–107, 109, 111
McVeigh, Timothy, 19
Metzger, Tom, 121
Michigan Socialist Party, 99
Miller, Richard, 101
Molland, Noel, 82
Moore, Roy, 48
Morrison, Adrian R., 71
Moussaoui, Zacarias, 163, 165–66
Mullins, Eustace, 129
Murad, Abdul Hakim, 163
Muslim Public Affairs council, 37
Muslim Student Association (MSA),
  35–37

Nelwert, David, 16
Newkirk, Ingrid, 74
Newton, Huey, 34–35
North, Gary, 49–50

Ogilvie, Matthew C., 18
Olympia Movement for Justice and
  Peace, 38–39
Orem, John, 75

Ostendorf, David, 27

Palestine Liberation Organization
  (PLO)
  terrorism and violence by, 168–71
    con, 175
Palestinian-Israeli dispute
  Arab Americans on, 44–46
Palestinians
  Israeli oppression of, 174, 175–76
  oppose violence, 174–75
  refugee problem of, 173
  two-state solution of, 173
  vision of peace by, 176
Paterson, Brian, 93
People for the Ethical Treatment of
  Animals (PETA), 70, 74, 75
Peres, Shimon, 168
Peters, Pete, 28–29
Phillips, Terry W., 135
Pierce, William, 31, 120
Pipes, Daniel, 36, 156
Podhoretz, Norman, 52
Posse Commitatus, 28
Potok, Mark, 13, 116–17
Pratkanis, Anthony, 13–14
Prestidge, John, 83

al Qaeda
  fighting, 160
  global network of, 159–60
  is an umbrella organization, 158–59
  procurement network in the West
    by, 158–59
  sponsorship for, 159
  threat by, 157–58
    is diminished, 162–64
Qatar Charitable Society, 159
Quincy, Illinois, 29
Quincy Ministerial Association, 29

racial profiling, Arab American
  support for, 44–45
racist Christian theologies
  countermodern suspicion by, 22–23
  fear of change by, 21–22
  on modern/liberal culture, 23–24
  must not be ignored, 29–31
  organized opposition is needed for,
    28–29
  progun lobby and, 20
  on racial segregation, 19–20
  religious leaders must stand against,
    31–32
  threat of, 19
  uses religion as a racist tool, 24–26
  violence by, 28
radical animal rights groups. *See*